CW01674289

HENLEY

PHYLLIS COURT CLUB

EX-LIBRIS

HELENA MAY –

THE PERSON, THE PLACE,

AND THE HISTORY IN HONG KONG

FEBRUARY 2016

HELENA MAY

The Person, The Place and 90 Years of History in Hong Kong

Written by

Esther Morris

with research by

The Helena May History Group

Helena May

The Person, The Place and
90 Years of History in Hong Kong

Dedicated to those for whom it was created
to provide a focus for women's benevolent
organisations, and as a refuge.

First published in Hong Kong in 2006
by The Helena May
35 Garden Road, Central, Hong Kong.

Copyright © 2006 by The Helena May

ISBN 988-99294-0-6
ISBN 978-988-99294-0-4

Designed by The Design Associates
Printed in Hong Kong

Contents

Map of Hong Kong 1880 vi

Patron's Foreword vii

The Helena May History Group viii

Acknowledgements ix

Preface xii

1. *Who was Helena May? Her Family and Hong Kong Connections* 1

2. *Pioneering Colonial Women and the Birth of the Helena May* 25

3. *The First 30 Years: 1916 to 1945* 45

4. *Post Second World War to the End of the Cultural Revolution* 69

5. *The Last 30 Years: 1977 to 2006* 99

Helena and Henry's Family Tree 114

Chronology of Events Related to the Helena May 115

List of Illustrations 116

Bibliography 118

Index 119

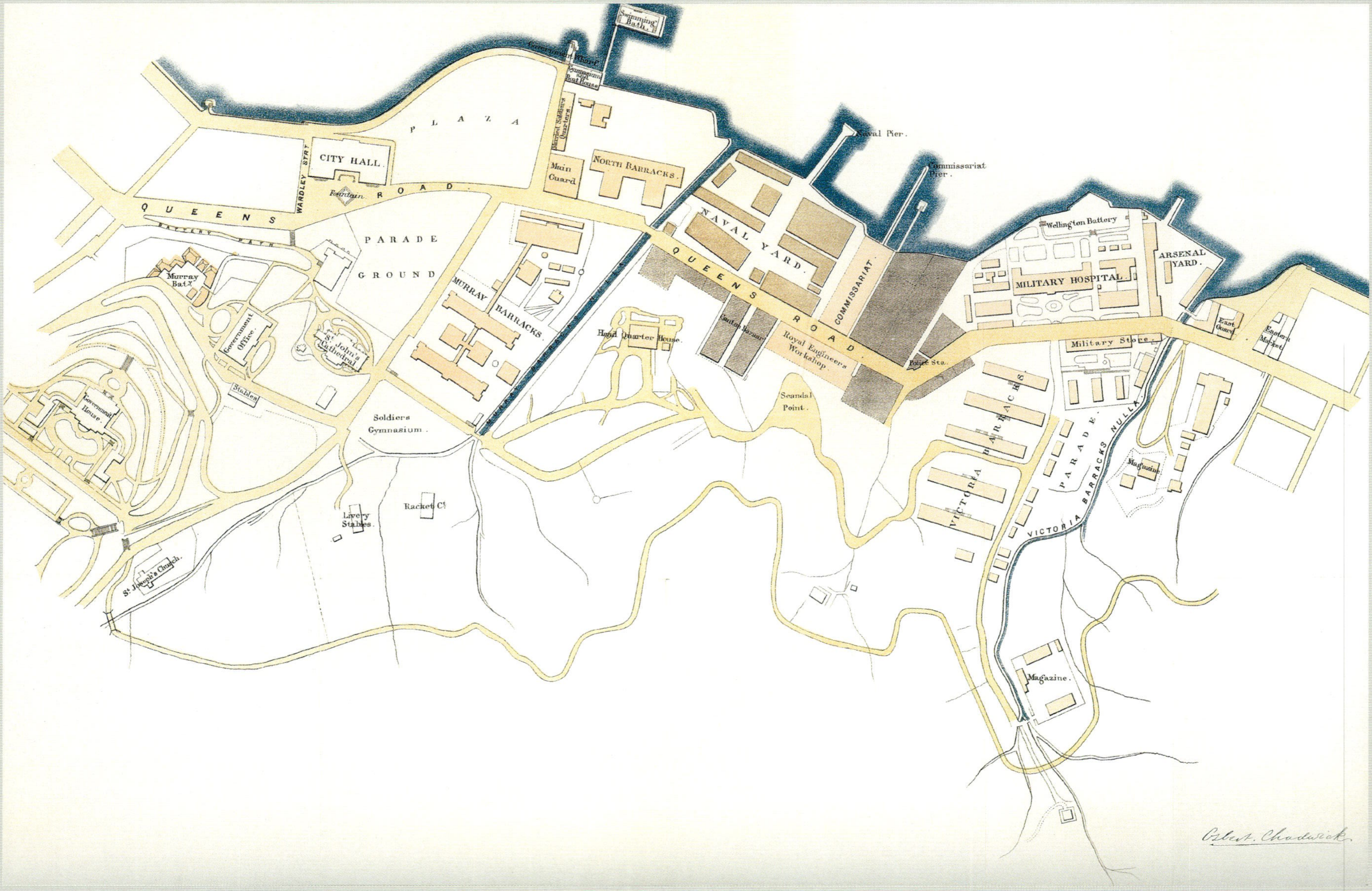
Swimming Bath.
Government Wharf
Gymnasium and Boat House
PLAZA
Married Soldiers Quarters
Main Guard
NORTH BARRACKS.
Naval Pier.
Commissariat Pier.
CITY HALL
WARDLEY STR
Fountain
QUEENS ROAD
BATTERY PATH
PARADE GROUND
NAVAL YARD.
COMMISSARIAT.
Wellington Battery
ARSENAL YARD.
MILITARY HOSPITAL.
Murray Batv.
Government Office.
St. John's Cathedral.
MURRAY BARRACKS.
Head Quarter House.
Canton Bazaar
Royal Engineers Workshop.
Police Sta.
Military Store.
East Guard
Eastern Market
Government House.
Stables
Soldiers Gymnasium.
Scandal Point.
VICTORIA BARRACKS
PARADE.
VICTORIA BARRACKS NULLA.
Magazine.
Racket Ct
Livery Stables.
St. Joseph's Church.
Magazine.
Osbert Chadwick

Foreword

I was delighted to be invited to be Patron of the Helena May. This honour came to me as wife of the Chief Executive of the Hong Kong Special Administrative Region. The Helena May Institute was founded in 1916 by Lady Helena May who was wife of the Governor of Hong Kong at that time. The Institute was inspired by a vision to provide accommodation for self-reliant ladies arriving in Hong Kong and a place for professional women to meet and work together in providing "social services in the community". The establishment of this lovely heritage building bearing her name on Garden Road realized that vision. After 90 years, the Institute is still fulfilling its original purpose. Over the years the Institute has matured with Hong Kong, witnessing momentous changes that have made Hong Kong a premier international city of Asia.

This book is a tribute to Lady Helena May, a woman who endeavoured to help both local and international women, and to all those who have drawn inspiration from her leadership. I am sure that members of the Helena May will continue to champion her spirit and carry on her mission in caring for the special needs of women and girls in Hong Kong.

Selina Tsang
Patron of the Helena May

The Helena May History Group

Elizabeth Cote, as Chairman of the Helena May in 2003, initiated the project by pointing out that the current recorded history ended in 1994, and that the booklet was nearly out of print. She brought people together to discuss what needed to be done, and researched and wrote the first draft of the history from 1995 to 2005. Her enthusiasm carried the project along until she left Hong Kong in March 2005.

Jenny Day researched the middle period – in particular those years spanning the Second World war – spending a great deal of time poring over microfiched newspapers. She also interviewed various people for memories and comments on the modern period and compiled the index. Most importantly she ensured that the manuscript had a designer and that everything on the publishing side was taken care of, thus guiding it through the final stages

Esther Morris researched a great deal of the history, edited and collated the work of other people, and wrote the final text. She also took part in interviews about the project and was involved in the final production stages.

Mary Painter did an enormous amount of work researching Helena's family history by corresponding with some of her grandchildren and visiting grandson Timothy Whitworth on several occasions. She continued this work even after she left Hong Kong in 2005 and personally delivered precious family photographs on a return trip.

* * *

Liz Latter researched the Council Minutes from 1946 before she left Hong Kong in 2005. She also helped with publicizing the project by being interviewed for a newspaper article and radio programme.

Jo Webb attended many meetings of the History Group and followed various avenues in an attempt to find out about the women who were involved with the Helena May in the early days. She also visited Helena's granddaughter, Veronica Johnston, in England in 2004. She too left Hong Kong in 2005.

Gill Townsend attended meetings and also supplied the interview with Dorothy Collins.

Marjorie Bray accompanied some of us on a visit to the Public Records Office and helped us to select photographs from the May Family Collection. She also talked to us about her own memories and links with Helena May's family.

Veronica Andrews, Debbie Chung, Jill Lander and Kate Williams attended early meetings of the History Group and contributed ideas.

ACKNOWLEDGEMENTS

This history owes a great deal to a large number of people and we are very grateful for all the time, effort and expertise that we have been able to draw upon. Our heartfelt thanks to all of the following:

First of all, there are the women who produced booklets that were entitled *A Short History of the Helena May*. The first booklet is dated 1934 and a reprint was made possible by the then Chairman, Agnes Wolfe, who sent a copy back to Hong Kong in 1946. There were updates in 1950, 1963, 1969, 1974 and 1979, which are all anonymous.

The most recent version, which included photographs and took the history up to 1994, was written by Robyn McLean of the Public Records Office and researched by Rosemary Lee, who was Vice-Chairman of Council at the time. It was the need to extend and expand this work that was the initial inspiration behind the present volume.

Several members of Helena May's family have generously helped with the project by supplying information and photographs through interviews and correspondence – in particular, Timothy Whitworth and Veronica Johnston, and also Margaret Osmaston, Mary Duncan, Andrew Whitworth, Lorna Headlam-Morley, Rachel Kinchin Smith and Alexandra Headlam-Morley.

Susanna Hoe's very thorough research has been drawn upon heavily in Chapter Two for much of the information about expatriate women in Hong Kong.

A number of people have read and commented on the text and been great supporters of the project: Marjory Bent, Geoffrey Bonsall, Peter Cunich, Colin Day, Staci Ford, Rodney Griffith, Paul Morris, Rebecca Morris, Catherine Robinson, Steve Vines and Jason Wordie.

Sue Gemmell supplied copies of programmes and articles featuring her grandparents, Aubrey Maurice and Katharine Marjory Bowes-Smith, who gave recitals in the 1930s; and Elizabeth Ride provided programmes of concerts in which her father, Sir Lindsay Ride, was singing.

Help has also been received at various stages and in various ways from the Antiquities and Monuments Office, Christopher Bailey *(Picture This Gallery)*, Kay Barker and Revd. Jenny Nam *(St Stephen's Girls' School)*, Gail Buttifant, Joan Campbell, Rachel Cartland, Joanne Chan *(Helena May Office)*, Annemarie Evans, Laurence Goldstein, Bernard Hui *(Public Records Office)*, Rosemary Inglis, Tom Kvan, Mrs Lee *(St Joseph's College)*; the National Archives at Kew *(UK)*, Betty Simpson *(Manager of the Helena May)*, Eva and Alistair Stewart, Fiona Tsang *(Hong Kong Museum of History)*, Ed Vickers, and the University of Hong Kong Library – especially Dr Y. C. Wan and Mrs Iris Chan.

Victor Cheong and Mia Yu of The Design Associates *(TDA)* have done a wonderful job in helping us to produce a book that we hope befits the people and the institution it is about.

The contemporary feature photographs were taken by Philip Suen and Mubaraka Ebrahim.

If anyone has been forgotten – you know what your contributions are – we thank you too.

PREFACE

Helena May was a lady deemed worthy of having an institution named after her – and not just because she was the wife of a Governor. She is an early example of the many expatriate women who have made a lasting contribution to Hong Kong through voluntary work. She had earned respect in the community – amongst both expatriates and locals – through her charity work and the force of her personality. As a result, she was able to attract the necessary donations to satisfy the need for a place that provided safe and comfortable accommodation for single European women, who were either working in or passing through Hong Kong, and from which other women could carry out community work.

The Helena May Institute was opened in 1916, but its history really begins with the birth of its namesake and encompasses the lives of several people who played important roles in the development of Hong Kong, including Helena's father, Major-General Digby Barker, her husband, Sir Francis Henry May, and the major benefactors, Sir Ellis Kadoorie and Ho Kom Tong. Those involved with the Helena May in 2006 also owe deep gratitude to Lucy Eyre – the lady who was a driving force behind its foundation – as well as the many women (and a few men) who have sustained the place over the decades and allowed it to be conserved for posterity.

Across Hong Kong there are currently 79 declared monuments that are permanently protected under the Antiquities and Monuments Ordinance (1976). As one of a small number of buildings of the British colonial era that has been preserved – with the exterior being declared a monument on 8 October 1993 – the Helena May is significant and can claim to be one of the few that is still fulfilling at least part of its original function. Several of the other 24 monuments on Hong Kong Island have links to Helena May and her family – Flagstaff House (formerly Headquarter House), Government House, the Gate Lodge of Mountain Lodge, St John's Cathedral, Central Police Station and Victoria Prison Compounds, the University of Hong Kong and St Stephen's Girls College.

The first chapter focuses on Helena and her family, in particular her father and husband and their careers in Hong Kong in the different important capacities in which they served.

The second chapter moves on to the contributions Helena, Lucy Eyre and other expatriate women made to the development of Hong Kong. It shows the need for and the eventual birth of the Helena May Institute, and the contributions made by the benefactors.

The third chapter starts the history of the institution itself and looks at developments during the first 30 years from the opening in 1916 up until the end of the Japanese Occupation. This is the section in which we have had to piece the history together as there are very few original records available. Unfortunately, in common with many other local institutions, much was lost during the Occupation, although the building itself was largely preserved.

The fourth chapter covers the next 30 years up to the end of the Cultural Revolution in China in 1976. This was the time when Hong Kong was being re-established as a British colony and then had other challenges to face.

The final chapter takes us up to the present. For both these latter periods we have been able to glean a great deal from Council records and the personal memories of members.

Women's lives in 2006 are very different from when Helena first set foot in Hong Kong in 1890 and made her impact over a period of 28 years. The Helena May has had to adapt over time, but as a place in which to live and meet it has been special for many people over its 90-year history. In bringing together this volume I am aware that we often have to rely on the interpretation of facts given by previous writers, and memories are not always accurate. We have tried to access as many sources as possible, but cannot claim that this is the definitive history of the Helena May. Its purpose is to remind readers of the original spirit and intentions of the people behind the place and to inspire others to carry on their work.

Esther Morris
July 2006

I. *Who was Helena May? Her Family and Hong Kong Connections*

Helena's Family Background

The girl who was to become Helena May was born in Scotland on 27 March 1863 – the year that the USA proclaimed the abolition of slavery and construction of the world's first underground railway in London began. As Helena Augusta Victoria Barker, she was the first of three children born to George Digby Barker and Frances (Fanny) Isabella Murray, who had married in June of the previous year.

At the time Helena's father was stationed at Edinburgh Castle with his regiment and her birth was registered at Newington, Midlothian, where the family were living. Helena was baptised at St Margaret's Chapel in Edinburgh Castle and named after her godmother – the young Princess Helena Augusta Victoria (1846-1923), fifth child and third daughter of Queen Victoria. An aunt in Frances' family had been governess to the princess, who consequently became a personal friend.

Helena's sister Mary Caroline (Carrie) was born in 1864 and her brother Digby Hildyard in 1865. The children were all privately educated, and the family lived the army life moving to various postings in England – Fareham, Portsmouth and Camberley.

The Barker family home was Clare Priory, a medium-sized country house with two small farms and picturesque gardens. Situated on the banks of the River Stour, it is on the edge of the medieval village of Clare in Suffolk – the English county north-east of London. The original Priory was established around 1248 for the Friars of the Order of St Augustine, but it passed into the hands of the Crown after the Reformation and became privately owned in the 16th century[1].

Along with nearby Clare Castle and Clare Hall, which sits on a rise overlooking the Stour valley, the Priory had belonged to the Barker family for several generations. Helena's father was born there in 1833, but left at the age of seven after his father died. His mother remarried and the family then moved to London. The Priory was let for 60 years as a school and then as a private home. Helena's father inherited it late in life because his elder brother died childless, and reoccupied it when he retired. Until 1953 it remained in the family and then was sold back to the Augustinians.

Helena in 1873

In contrast, Helena's mother's family had a home at the other end of Britain near Hill of Fearn, Easter Ross – a quiet and lonely place a little way from the northern shore of the Moray Firth in the far north-east of Scotland. It is thus likely that Frances met George in Edinburgh.

Helena's Father and Moving to Hong Kong

Following a distinguished military career that began in 1853, including service in the Persian campaign and Indian Mutiny (which are described in his *Letters from Persia and India 1857 – 1859: A Subaltern's Experiences in War*, edited by Lady Barker in 1915), Helena's father spent some time in military education and was promoted to Major-General in 1887. Having been awarded Companion of the Order of the Bath (CB) in 1889, he was called to serve as British Commanding Officer in China and Hong Kong.[2] Thus in 1890, when Helena was 27 years old, the family followed in the footsteps of millions of other British people before them who had gone to live and work in the colonies[3] and moved to Hong Kong.

The military barracks on Hong Kong Island were extensive and there was a hospital and a swimming pool on the waterfront as well as the Naval Yard. The family would have lived in Headquarter House in Victoria Barracks, and close by were St John's Cathedral, Government House and City Hall – places that would cater to their spiritual and cultural needs and figure prominently in the family's history in Hong Kong.

The formal order of precedence of the time was Governor, Commander-in-Chief, Admiral, Bishop, Chief Justice, Colonial Secretary and Attorney General. Thus Helena's father, as number two in this chain, was in a very powerful and privileged position. *The Hong Kong Telegraph* of 5 April 1891 reports that Barker was in the party that was invited by Prince Nikolai Alexandrovitch of Russia on board his yacht during his visit to Hong Kong.[4] Three years later the prince became Tsar Nicholas II, and in 1918 he was assassinated along with other members of his family.

Due to the failing health of Governor Sir William Des Voeux, Barker was Acting Governor of the colony from 7 May to 10 December 1891. (It was during this period that Helena married Henry May, as we shall see later.) Barker's role was especially onerous as he had not been a member of the Legislative Council and was unfamiliar with its procedures. *The Hong Kong Daily Press* in a review of the year states:

...the reins of government passed into the hands of Major-General Barker, who held them with firmness and discretion during a time of exceptional difficulty, until the arrival of (the next Governor, Sir William) Robinson.[5]

According to the record of the Legislative Council meeting of 15 October 1891, the ordinances being dealt with by the government at this time included those relating to the importation of opium, smuggling, the necessity for more space for interment, gambling, auxiliary defence, squatters, and the construction of a new prison due to overcrowding. Just before the end of his term in office Barker also had to deal with the ongoing concerns of the Chamber of Commerce about the rising costs of the administration and the growth of the Civil Service, which was deemed to be due to the need to find jobs for the stream of cadets coming into the colony from Britain.[6]

FLAGSTAFF HOUSE Built as Headquarter House in Victoria Barracks in 1846 for Major General George Charles D'Aguilar, this is often deemed to be the oldest existing Western-style building in Hong Kong. (In fact a Chapel had been built in the Colonial Cemetery nine months previously and can still be seen in what is now the Hong Kong Cemetery.) It was renamed Flagstaff House in 1932, and was used by Japanese troops during the Occupation. Subsequently it remained the residence of the Commander of British Forces until 1978, when the Commander moved to a purpose-built house on Barker Road.

In 1979 it was handed over to the Government and in early 1984 it became the Museum of Tea Ware, displaying Chinese tea ware and related material of different periods. It was declared a monument in 1989. Part of Victoria Barracks became Hong Kong Park and was opened to the public in May 1991. The K. S. Lo Gallery was added to the Museum in 1995.

A small insight into the characters of the Barkers is provided by Herbert James, a major in the Army Medical Service, who recounts in December 1892 that he had called on Mrs Barker and that she seemed 'a nice woman'. He had also met the General at dinner and describes him as 'a miniature man with a considerable carpet-bag, but pleasant.'[7]

Barker remained in his post until 1895, when he handed over to General Black and left to be Governor of the Bermudas until early 1902. In recognition of his services in Hong Kong, and following common practice at the time to name roads after military leaders in the colony, Barker Road was gazetted on 5 November 1898. Helena's sister, who became known as Aunt Carrie, married a soldier, Major General James Cecil Dalton, in 1899. In the same year Helena's brother, Digby, who had become a captain in the army, died. And in the following year her mother also died.

It was in 1900 that Barker received a knighthood and soon afterwards returned to England for his retirement. He served as a Justice of the Peace in Essex and Suffolk and in 1902 married the much younger Katherine (Katie) Weston Elwes, with two of the May girls as bridesmaids at the wedding. In her book *View from the Peak*, written originally in the 1960s, Helena's second daughter Phoebe describes Katie, whom the children referred to as 'Donna', as 'a pretty cousin' and 'a very dear relation' who was 'a superb housekeeper and homemaker' at Clare Priory, which she helped to restore to its former glory.[8] Katie's uncle, William Allen Whitworth, was the vicar of the church in London in which she was married, and 23 years later Phoebe married the vicar's second son, George Whitworth, who himself became vicar of Great St Mary's Church in Market Place, Cambridge. After a long and fulfilled life, George Digby Barker died on 15 April 1914 and Helena inherited the Priory, her brother having died childless.

HELENA'S HUSBAND

Francis Henry May was born on 14 March 1860 in Dublin, the fifth of ten children of the Rt. Hon George A. C. May, who became Lord Chief Justice of Ireland (1877-1887), and Olivia Barrington. Her family came from Limerick

Helena just before she came to Hong Kong

HONG KONG CADETS The special class of civil servants called Administrative Officers evolved from the Cadet Service, which had been introduced by Governor Sir Hercules Robinson (Lord Rosmead) in 1861. The main requirement was that these men should be able to learn Chinese in order to communicate effectively with the local population. They were 'an administrative corps d'elite: a minuscule band of officials with the same values and from the same social background'.

Out of the 85 cadets appointed between 1862 and 1941, Henry was one of the few with outstanding academic records, and the first of only three who eventually became Governors of Hong Kong – the other two being Sir Cecil Clementi (1925-1930) and Sir Alexander Grantham (1947-1957).

CENTRAL POLICE STATION AND VICTORIA PRISON The original prison was built in 1841, the first Western building constructed of durable material in Hong Kong. Most of the buildings within the compound were damaged by bombing during the Second World War. The Prison was reopened in 1946 after repairs and remained in use until 2005.

The oldest structure within the police station compound is a barrack block built in 1864. It is a three-storey building constructed adjacent to Victoria Prison. A further storey was added to the block in 1905. In 1919, Headquarters Block facing Hollywood Road was constructed. Subsequently, in 1925, the two-storey Stable Block was constructed at the north-west end of the parade ground and later used as an armoury. The compound was declared a monument in 1995 and was used by the Hong Kong Police Force until 2005. It then became the source of much debate as to its future – an issue that had not been resolved at the time of writing.

and lived there in Glenstal Castle, which was turned into a Benedictine Abbey and boys' boarding school in the 1920s.

The May family has an impressive genealogy, and Henry's father was one of the most distinguished members with a double first from Magdalene College, Cambridge. Two of Henry's brothers were knighted for their contributions to different professions – Edward as a soldier and Gould as a doctor. Of his three sisters, Charlotte Phoebe and Stella Millicent never married, but their names lived on in two of Helena and Henry's daughters, Stella and Phoebe. Michael, son of their fourth daughter, Dione, produced a history of the Irish Mays in 1992. Using Charlotte Phoebe's diary as a reference, he describes the Mays as being a 'privileged but happy family in the hey-day of late Victorian prosperity'.[9]

Henry's schooling was at Harrow in England and from there he proceeded to Trinity College, Dublin, where he studied classics and modern languages and was awarded first class honours in his BA degree in 1881. After taking the requisite competitive examination, he was appointed as a Cadet Officer in the Colonial Service in November of the same year.[10] He was sent to Peking to study Mandarin for two years before being attached to the Colonial Secretary's Office in Hong Kong. He continued studying and passed his final examination in 1885. He also learnt Cantonese and along with his Chinese teacher compiled *A Guide to Cantonese Colloquial*.[11]

Having worked his way through the ranks in various government departments, by April 1886 Henry was Assistant Registrar-General and in January 1891 he was made Assistant Colonial Secretary. While Helena's father was Acting Governor that year, Henry was made his private secretary, and it was during this period that he and Helena became engaged. Phoebe notes that the family were often shown 'the exact spot on the roof of Government House' where Henry proposed.[12] Mary Duncan, daughter of Helena and Henry's eldest daughter, Stella, recalls her grandmother telling her that she had never been allowed to be in a room alone with Henry up until the time they became engaged.

It must have been a short engagement for Helena, then aged 28, and Henry, aged 31, as they were married on 31 August 1891 at St John's Cathedral. Helena's sister and two daughters of the Hon. J. J. Keswick of Jardine Matheson Company acted as bridesmaids. William Goodman, a judge who was acting as Colonial Secretary, attended the wedding. In his memoirs he calls Henry an 'able man' and 'a very valuable helper' during this period. He also comments that the Mays were always 'most friendly' with him and his wife.[13]

HENRY AND HELENA'S UPWARD PROGRESS

Helena affectionately called her husband 'Hal', though he called himself 'Frank' in his personal correspondence and was also known as 'Paddy', because of his Irish origins. In documents he is referred to by both his Christian names, though most often 'Henry'. During the hot summer months they rented a house called Bahar Lodge at 28 Mount Austin Road, 1600 feet up on the Peak. Their first daughter, Stella, was born there in 1892.

Henry came to particular prominence after 1893 when he was appointed Captain Superintendent of Police and Fire Brigade and of Victoria Gaol: '... an appointment that was to have extensive ramifications... (as he) set to work like a whirlwind.'[14] Along with other duties, Henry also sat on the equivalent of the Urban Council and on the Legislative Council. He and Helena then lived in the official quarters at the Central Police Station in the city of Victoria. In her memoir Phoebe comments:

It cannot have been a very salubrious place to bring up young children, surrounded as it was by Chinese dwellings and only a few minutes' walk from the crowded and noisy main streets of the town.[15]

The police force at that time comprised European, Sikh and Chinese units, and Henry had the difficult task of welding them together to create 'an efficient armed constabulary'.[16] He is also remembered for creating a rural police organization and for 'the vigorous purge with which he expelled corrupt elements from the urban force'.[17] In spring 1894, after a winter so cold that ice formed on the Peak, and whilst China was at war with Japan, Henry had a major problem to deal with in the colony – the first bubonic plague.[18] This allowed him to demonstrate his skills as a leader and gave the police force an opportunity to earn respect in the community.[19]

A more pleasant aspect of life for Henry and Helena was hosting the children's Christmas treat in the large police station compound, which in those days possessed a lawn. According to a newspaper report of 12 January 1895,[20] the

Bahar Lodge at centre

BUBONIC PLAGUE In the early days of the Colonial Administration there was no law requiring the registration of deaths in the Chinese community, and temples were used to store dead bodies until an appropriate time and place, according to the rituals of feng shui, could be found for burial. In May 1894, as the temperatures rose and the rat population increased, fever was spreading through the slums of Tai Ping Shan at the western side of Victoria. This area had been known as a sanctuary for Chinese criminals and European down-and-outs and was rebuilt in subsequent years.

Major-General Barker placed some of the British Forces' doctors at the disposal of the government, and some 300 officers and men formed what became known as the 'whitewash brigade', though their efforts were not welcomed by the local population. Police Officers acted as interpreters, as the Europeans amongst them could speak Chinese and some of the Chinese police could speak English.

Over the next few months 2,500 people died and life in the colony was severely disrupted as disputes raged over the competing merits of Chinese and Western medicine. 100,000 fled to the Chinese countryside. The first of the Tung Wah Group of Hospitals, one of Hong Kong's powerful institutions, was established and people learned of the need to boil drinking water and avoid uncooked food.

event involved flat and obstacle races and a tug-of-war, followed by tea and the dispensing of presents by Santa Claus. Among other guests were Helena's parents and sister.

However, in March of the same year Henry and the police force had to deal with 20,000 coolies going on strike for more than a month, and causing havoc to the interests of the port. In recognition of all his efforts he was honoured as a Companion of the Order of St Michael and St George (CMG).

Family and social life

Although a member of the Legislative Council, Henry was actually on leave for part of 1895. It was inevitable that expatriates would be away from Hong Kong for several months at a time because of the long journeys by ship to and from Britain. These long absences amongst civil servants were one of the things that the Chamber of Commerce had been complaining about during Barker's time as Acting Governor.

It was during that family trip to Europe that Phoebe May was born at the Murray family home in Scotland. The doctor who delivered her came from the nearby village of Portmahomack and remembered the family well when Helena went to visit him on a return trip 18 years later after the family had been playing golf and having a picnic.[21]

Besides his interest in languages, Henry was also a great sportsman. He had been an amateur jockey when a young man and enjoyed cricket, golf, hunting, fishing, rifle shooting, polo and yachting. He was Commodore of The Royal Hong Kong Yacht Club from 1896 to 1904, and is known to have owned, at different times, boats named Kitten and Dione.[22] The latter won championship races in 1903, 1905, 1906 and 1908.[23] He encouraged the development of a golf course at Fanling, made sure the reservoirs were stocked with fish, was a member of the eight-team cricket league that existed from 1903, and won trophies at polo. He even wrote books on horse racing and sailing.

Most photographs show Henry as a serious man, and this was confirmed after he retired in a tribute paid to him by Legislative Councillor Lau Chu-pak (who was also one of the original benefactors of the Helena May): 'Sparing of speech and sparing of smiles, he never spared himself in the execution of his duty to the colony'.[24]

However, as Phoebe notes in her book, the children knew him very differently. He was not stern enough in the opinion of his brother, Gould, when Phoebe did something wrong and she remembers how he 'just looked… with his large eyes and solemn buffalo expression, and said nothing'. He very much enjoyed

playing with the girls, organizing games and sing-songs and playing practical jokes, as well as teaching them 'to sail, ride, know the stars, love nature and even to cook on a Chinese chatty'. He could tell Irish stories 'in a rich brogue which brought the house down', and 'was full of ideas and loved what he called a ploy'.[25]

The children of members of the police force, who were entertained at an annual New Year party at the Central Police Station, also saw this softer side of Henry. In a newspaper report of 9 January 1897, the Mays and other ladies and gentlemen are described as 'gaily frolicking with the little ones and doing all they possibly could to make the enjoyment thorough'.[26]

Helena and Henry's third daughter, Iris, who lived longest of the four girls, was born at Bahar Lodge in 1898. This was a significant year because the British acquired the New Territories on a 99 year lease. It was the ending of this lease that brought about the reunification of Hong Kong with Mainland China in 1997.

In 1900, while the Boxer Rebellion was in progress in China, the Mays built a house of their own on the Peak on the steep hillside overlooking the harbour and close to the Tram Station. They called it Ligoniel*, after a property owned by the May family in Ireland. Dione, the fourth daughter, was born there in the same year. Although the youngest of the children, she was the first to die at the age of 63.

* The spelling is also recorded as 'Ligoneil' in some correspondence.

Because of their father's interest in languages the girls had a German governess. Other staff at the house were Chinese and included a houseboy, nursery boy, house coolie, cook, cook's mate, washerman and tailor – all of whom lived in the adjoining coolies' quarters.[27]

In 1901, the Young Men's Christian Association (YMCA) was founded in Hong Kong with Henry as one of its leading promoters. He continued to sponsor the institution throughout his time in Hong Kong and acted as President.[28] Meanwhile the May family went to England on leave for a year and stayed at a house belonging to Helena's father at Camberley in Surrey. This was an opportunity for the girls to meet other family members and attend their grandfather's wedding. It was at this time, according to Phoebe's memoir, that she and Stella joined the Ministering Children's League, which had been set up 'to encourage children of the leisured classes to do good'.[29] It had been founded in 1884 in London by Lady Meath, whose estate was also in Surrey.[30]

View of the Peak Tram with a house on the left

BACK TO GOVERNMENT HOUSE

On their return to Hong Kong in autumn 1902, Henry became Colonial Secretary and in November 1903 he took over from Sir Henry Blake as Acting Governor, though:

...(He) did not share his departing master's enthusiasm for radical changes in China, was deeply antipathetic to revolutionaries and suspicious – often with good reason – of their approaches to the Governor... (Thus) May immediately took advantage of his new position to undo some of the late Governor's work by pushing through the Peak Reservation Ordinance, which was designed to exclude non-Europeans from that favoured area.[31]

MOUNTAIN LODGE This castle-like building had been constructed in the style of the Scottish Lodges. With its manicured lawns, tennis courts and shrubberies, it had been the Governor' s summer residence on top of the Peak since 1867.

The Lodge the May family lived in was its third incarnation, the second having been demolished in 1897. Apparently they were never well built and suffered from the humid climate. The last one was finally demolished in 1946.

However, the Gate Lodge on Mount Austin Road, which was built in the Renaissance style between 1900 and 1902 as living quarters for the keeper of Mountain Lodge, has been preserved and was declared a monument in 1995.

However, the Governor-General in Council had some discretion and the prominent Jardine, Matheson and Company comprador Sir Robert Ho Tung was allowed to live on the Peak, though he would probably not have wished to join the Peak Club, which was a centre for tea dances and bridge parties before dinner, and described as 'Surbiton or Wimbledon, in an atmosphere as truly British as roast beef or muffins'.[32]

Government House thus became Helena's home for the second time – though this time she was the mistress. The children then saw little of their parents, 'who were always entertaining, opening bazaars, laying foundation stones, making speeches and attending committee meetings' notes Phoebe.[33] However, in the hot weather at least, the family had a change of scene when they moved to Mountain Lodge.

On the Peak, drying rooms were vital to combat mildew, and Phoebe comments that she and her sisters even kept their favourite dolls in one of them 'for fear of their wigs'. However, in order to produce the required heat for this luxury of expatriate life, Chinese coolies had to deliver a constant supply of coal, which they carried up the mountain in the traditional fashion with two baskets balanced on a pole across their shoulders.

In July of the year that the tramways opened (1904), Sir Matthew Nathan arrived in Hong Kong for his short stint as Governor. He is described as 'a man of fine, upstanding presence' with 'a happy, courteous manner' though 'inept in personal relationships'.[34] He was Jewish, two years younger than Henry, and remained a bachelor.[35] Thus Helena, as the senior lady in the colony, took the lead in social matters pertaining to the Governor, while Henry was given a free hand to use his 25 years of experience in various government matters. Nathan was very kind to the May daughters, and they were a ready-made family for him.[36] Phoebe recalls how they performed a play at Government House at his request.

Mountain Lodge and the Gate Lodge 1912

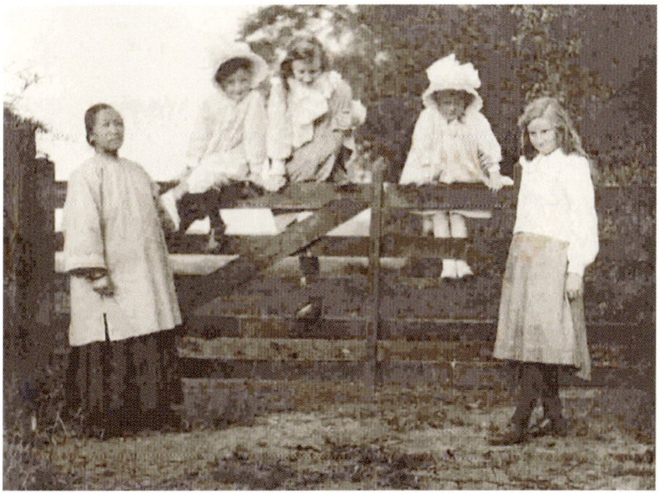

Helena and the girls went on long leave in the spring of 1905 taking the six-week sea journey on a P & O steamer. They stayed at the farmhouse, Clare Hall, where Henry joined them in the autumn. It was during the winter that Phoebe met the boy who was to become her husband 20 years later – George Whitworth. The family returned to Hong Kong in the autumn of 1906, though Stella remained at school in England.

1906 was a terrible year in different parts of the world. In San Francisco there was a severe earthquake, and in Hong Kong the Observatory gave little warning of a devastating typhoon that caused the loss of more than 11,000 lives and 41 merchant ships to be driven ashore. Among those who died was the Anglican Bishop Hoare, who had been trying to save trainees on his mission vessel.[37] Meanwhile, in the same year many Chinese in Hong Kong were reported to be opium smokers. However, the government reaped hefty revenue from the sales and so was not inclined to change the situation.[38] Life was pleasanter for the May girls as they attended society weddings.

Governor Nathan is remembered by Nathan Road in Tsimshatsui, and Henry was also honoured by having a road named after him. The Government Gazette notice of 12 April 1907 notes: 'The new road now in course of construction from Magazine Gap Road... to the Peak Road at Queen's Gardens shall henceforth be known as May Road'.[39] With the development and production of cars more proper roads were needed. The first imports came in 1908 and Henry was among the early owners in Hong Kong. As a result, sedan chairs were increasingly abandoned.

ANOTHER NEW GOVERNOR

When Sir Frederick and Lady Lugard arrived in Hong Kong on 28 July 1907, they were met by the Mays as Henry was still Colonial Secretary. Lady Lugard was formerly Flora Shaw, and Joanna Trollope notes that among the women who gave 'dutiful service to the Empire' Flora is 'so remarkable that she must be placed in a category quite her own'.[40]

Lugard's biographer, Margery Perham[41] quotes the 55 year old Flora as saying: 'Mrs. May was pretty, thoroughly human and full of sense – one of the sort one takes to at sight', and of Henry, Lugard says '... a desperate keen sportsman and as hard as nails. I like him very much, he is white right through'.

Photograph in England 1905 at Clare Hall – the daughters and Ah Soo (Sooey)

In various letters he writes 'The Colonial Secretary is a demi-god and his office runs the show' and 'a strong man... (who) commands the respect of all'.[42]

Perham goes on to note what life was like for the Lugards in Hong Kong, and thus gives a flavour of the times:

The entertaining was an essential part of governing Hong Kong. Government House was used as a high-class hotel, restaurant and sports club by many of the hundreds of passengers who left their ships to write their names in the Governor's book... there were the British official visitors, generals and admirals on tours of inspection, diplomats and experts of many kind. Socially most exacting were the many distinguished foreigners and Eastern potentates – Chinese and Japanese princes, Indian Rajahs, the Governor of neighbouring Portuguese Macao, foreign admirals who had to be visited in their warships and later entertained in turn at Government House; ambassadors en route to or from Tokyo or Peking, and many lesser functionaries. The official, commercial and Chinese residents of Hong Kong were always with them, presenting delicate problems of hospitality in an artificial community, in a day when class division was still almost unchallenged and official hierarchy was exactly reflected in social life... Hong Kong's few thousand Europeans were not only divided horizontally into an number of classes, but perpendicularly divided according to profession. There were battalions of soldiers to be welcomed, inspected or sent off; merchants in their Chambers of Commerce and other societies; associations of engineers and many other professions. There were all the different religious sects with an astonishing number of institutions of every kind run by them which had to be opened, visited, aided through concerts or bazaars or have their prizes given out... Then there were all the scores of sporting clubs and events... not to speak of dramatic clubs and chrysanthemum societies.[43]

Despite constant poor health due to earlier bouts of malaria, Lady Lugard refurbished the official residences and entertained 'wonderfully and imaginatively'[44] – thus no doubt inspiring the future Lady May. A recurring matter that Lugard had to face was how to control the opium trade. The British Parliament had been condemning it for many years and in 1908 sent instructions for opium divans to be closed. The Hong Kong Government's concern focused on the effect this would have on the economy, and Lugard pointed out that the number of addicts had dwindled to 14,000 and the divans were more like social clubs. Henry lent support to the argument by saying that he had visited many divans and had not seen anyone 'worse for the drug'. Indeed he himself had 'smoked many pipes in succession with no result.'[45] Although the divans were closed the trade continued, as the purchase and consumption of opium remained lawful.

A more positive and major development under Lugard's governorship was the founding of the University of Hong Kong, as a British style university for Chinese students to assist in the modernisation of China. It had been preceded by the College of Medicine, of which Henry was Rector.

Sir Henry and Lady May

In the summer of 1909, Henry took leave with the family in Canada, where he could indulge his passion for fishing. Towards the end of the year, he was named by Edward VII in his birthday honours list as Knight Commander of the Most Distinguished Order of St Michael and St George (KCMG). According to the *South China Weekly Post*,[46] which extended congratulations in an article about Henry's career, this order was '... specially for natural born subjects who have held, or are likely to hold, high and confidential offices within His Majesty's Colonial possessions; and in reward of services to the Crown in relation to the foreign affairs of the Empire'. In the article it is noted that Henry had declined the Colonial Secretaryship of Ceylon 'preferring to return to the scene of so many years of his life's labour'. Some people said that he had been hoping to be made Governor in succession to Lugard. Lady May is described as 'one of the most popular ladies of the colony'. Another article is even more fulsome in its praise:

In all forms of philanthropic work in the colony, Lady May has taken a most active share ever since she arrived in Hong Kong, and there can be but few among the many charities and good works set on foot locally which have not at one time or another come within the sphere of her generous activities.[47]

Phoebe[48] quotes a letter written on 9 November 1909 by Sir Frederick Lugard:

My dear May,
I have just written a line to congratulate Lady May on the title you have earned for her by some 26 years of honest good work for your country. I am quite sure that the chief pleasure that this promotion gives you is the pretty honour it confers on your wife, and I shall not detract from your own merit when I say that she equally deserves it for all she has done in this Colony, and – far above any particular thing that she has done – for the tone she has set, and the example of generosity and liberal mindedness which is intolerant of petty jealousies. The good that such an example confers is not measurable, it is an unconscious asset to the Colony, of which it never appreciates the value till it loses it. When she goes with you to a new Colony she will bring the same sweet influence to Government House there.

The following year was a 'golden age' in Phoebe's recollection. She was reading Shakespeare, going to concerts and organ recitals, and becoming more involved in visits to missionary schools and orphanages. It was the year of the accession of King George V and Henry became Acting Governor again. The family moved into Mountain Lodge for another six months and life continued with afternoon teas and tennis, visits to sandy beaches and Sunday School.

Cecil Clementi was Henry's Private Secretary and the May daughters played with Dorothy Eyres, who was the youngest daughter of the Naval Commodore, and whose elder sister, Penelope, eventually married Cecil, who became Governor in 1925.[49] Stella, now 18 years old, returned to Hong Kong in the autumn and joined in 'the happy atmosphere that Mummy created'.[50]

Despite unfavourable weather, on 1 October 1910, the 22 mile long single-tracked British Section of the Kowloon-Canton Railway from Tsim Sha Tsui to Lo Wu was formally opened by Henry, and he along with Helena, their daughters and other dignitaries were the first passengers to travel on it. This major event in the history of the colony is described at length in a newspaper column of the day and was cause for great celebration. Work on the railway had commenced in 1906, and continued over the next few years as more sections were opened. The railway was deemed to be an asset whose worth would 'defy calculation' and almost rival the harbour itself in its potential for the development of Hong Kong by establishing a land link for trade with China and beyond. The recently acquired New Territories became easily accessible, and the expatriate community in particular took advantage of the opportunity to visit the area.[51]

Towards the end of 1910 came the news that Henry was to be appointed Governor of Fiji and High Commissioner for the Western Pacific – with only five weeks notice. Not everyone was happy about this appointment. Apparently James Lockhart, who had been Colonial Secretary prior to Henry and thus his senior, saw it as a promotion over his head.[52]

Phoebe tells how a presentation was made to Helena in the City Hall a few days before they left by some elderly Chinese residents – but only gentlemen, as it was not the custom for wives to come to public functions in those days. The gifts of jade, ivory, embroidery and teacups on a silver stand were in recognition of Helena's 'kindness, courtesy and gentleness.' In order to respect the Chinese way of doing things, which the Mays much admired and were very

Henry and Helena with daughters. (From left) Stella, Dione, Iris and Phoebe. c.1910.

sensitive to, Henry made the thank you speech on Helena's behalf – though no doubt she would have been very capable of doing it herself.

Ligoniel and most of its contents were sold as an annexe to the Peak Hotel, which was located in Victoria Gap next to the Upper Peak Tramway Terminus and remained open until 1937. The May family left Hong Kong on 21 January 1911. Phoebe gives a lot of details of their stay in Fiji in her memoir, together with the fact that they took all of their Chinese household staff with them, including their full-time tailor. Many years later, Helena made a return trip to Fiji and discovered that two of their former staff had established thriving businesses.

Back in Hong Kong

In March 1912, Henry was cabled from Downing Street (the Prime Minister's headquarters in London) that he was to leave Fiji and go back to Hong Kong as the 15th Governor. Phoebe describes their return in July and notes how the Chinese servants, in line with the stewards on the ship they were travelling on, had cut off their queues (pigtails) – symbols of Manchu domination – because of the overthrow of the Chinese empire:

It was because of the revolution that Daddy had been so unexpectedly recalled to Hong Kong after only fifteen months. The authorities at the Colonial Office felt it was necessary to have a man who understood China and the Chinese people.[53]

She goes on to describe the warm welcome the family received as they disembarked at Blake Pier, including the 17 gun salute, guard of honour and military band. 'Picturesque' and 'imperturbable' chair coolies were ready with the special scarlet curtained Government House sedan chairs to take them all to City Hall for the continuation of the ceremonies and Sikh policemen formed an escort. However, Hong Kong was a much changed place with the advent of the Republic in China, and an incident affecting the Mays demonstrated this. A local newspaper reported:

On July 4, 1912, the newly-appointed Governor arrived here on his return from Fiji and a great reception was arranged. Sir Henry and Lady May, accompanied by their four daughters, landed at Blake Pier and entered the state sedan chairs for the ceremonial procession to the City Hall, where addresses of welcome were to be presented. Shortly after the procession started, and when the chairs had arrived opposite what is known today as Union Building (which later became Swire House and is now Chater Building) a Chinese stepped forward from the crowd and fired a revolver. The bullet passed close to the Governor, going under the awning of his chair, and lodged in the chair occupied by Lady May, where it was subsequently found.[54]

The events are recorded by the Acting Colonial Secretary, A. M. Thomson, in his report in the *Blue Book for the Year 1912*:

As the new Governor was proceeding from the landing place to the City Hall, he was fired at by a Chinese, who rushed up to the Governor's chair and discharged a revolver close to Sir Henry May's face. The man was seized by the prompt action of serjeant (sic) Garrod and Indian police constable Kala Singh. The man alleged as his motive a grievance on account of the prohibition of the circulation in Hong Kong of foreign copper coins, and of the repatriation of Chinese from South Africa.

Typically, history is a matter of interpretation of events and another account notes that:

The wretched would-be assassin was seized by the crowd and manhandled so badly that his clothes were described as being "in tatters" by the time he arrived at the nearest police station. It transpired that the man's father had been imprisoned on corruption charges at the time when Sir Henry was Superintendent of Police and the attempted assassination was an act of vengeance on behalf of his father. The man was sent to prison, like his father, and the Governor got a motor-car to travel in instead of the rather more exposed sedan chairs.[55]

Yet another writer names the gunman as Li Hong-hung, and says that he 'was believed to harbour a grudge against May from his days in the police... (but) It could also have been prompted by the increasing chaos in China'. However, in a letter dated 11 August 1912 to the *Times* correspondent in Peking, Australian adventurer Dr G. E. Morrison, May himself records that it was just a misunderstanding:

The attack on me has no political significance at all. The man was I am sure crazy, although the doctors who examined him at my instance pronounced him sane. Curiously enough he mixed up Fiji with South Africa (Feichau in Cantonese) and thought I was the governor of the Transvaal and had turned his compatriots out of that country.[57]

Whatever the truth about the incident, it was certain that officials wished to play it down and not cause further antagonism. Phoebe notes that no-one mentioned it at the lunch at Government House which followed the swearing-in ceremony. Her own interests lay in moving again to Mountain Lodge for the summer – and going there on a special Peak Tram, which had eyes painted on the front according to a Chinese custom.

Henry was keen to demonstrate that all was well and went into town the next day with only his ADC in attendance. Phoebe recalls: 'They returned some hours later having perambulated the busiest and most congested streets in China town and we were greatly relieved to have them safely back'. The prisoner was released after two years, on condition that he leave Hong Kong and never return. Phoebe recalls the moving scene as her father relayed this order and the man was reunited with his daughter.

Hong Kong under Henry's Governorship

In September 1912, Henry became the second Chancellor of the University of Hong Kong – an honorary position held by the Governor – and also continued as Rector of the College of Medicine, until its dissolution in 1915. He served on various committees of the University, and his contribution was recognized by the third hostel on the main campus being named May Hall. The first hostel had been named after Lugard and the second after Charles Eliot, the first Vice-Chancellor, who took the post after it had been declined by Cecil Clementi.[58] The three-storey red-brick Edwardian-style buildings on terraces were linked by corridors and stairs. They were designed by the Architects Messrs Denison, Ram and Gibbs, who also designed The Helena May Institute.

The following March, Helena and the children left Hong Kong for home leave in Britain – staying in London and visiting Helena's father. Henry joined then in September for a holiday in Ireland and to play golf near the Murray family home in Scotland. When the family returned to Hong Kong in November, Henry and Stella travelled by Trans-Siberian railway rather than by ship. Meanwhile, Phoebe stayed behind in England and spent Christmas with Aunt Carrie at The Hutts – the home she and her husband had retired to in the village of Grewelthorpe, north-west of Ripon in North Yorkshire. Thereafter Phoebe went to Paris for six months to finish her education.

Being away from Hong Kong was an especially good idea at this time. A newspaper reported in April 1913 on the problem of plague: 'Officer of Health Dr Francis Clark told the Sanitary Board there had been a large increase in the number of rats; his office had collected 86,933 dead rodents the previous year. The only way to contain plague was to deny them food, he said angrily, but continued: 'There are tenants in the city, Europeans as well as Chinese, who make no attempt to maintain their premises in rat-proof condition.' The following month saw a further 185 plague deaths, taking the toll to 1,301, and the city was not declared plague-free until October.[59]

As noted above, Henry was amongst the first to have a car in Hong Kong at a time when 'the streets were choked with bullock carts, trams, rickshaws, sedan chairs and horses' and 'outside Central there were only 15 kilometres of carriage road, from Aberdeen to North Point, until a public-works programme saw the building round Hong Kong Island of a road for motor vehicles. It reached Deep Water Bay in 1915 and Repulse Bay in 1917, and completed the circle over the new Tai Tam Dam in 1918'.[60]

Also in 1913 Henry became concerned with local education and pronounced it 'chaotic'. He thus introduced a Bill to bring the vernacular schools under the supervision of the Director of Education, who was given the power to close inefficient schools. All of the 620 schools with their 11,909 pupils were required to be registered.[61]

One of the visitors the Mays entertained in early 1914 was former Times correspondent G. E. Morrison, who had been resident in China since 1897 and had witnessed both the end of the Qing dynasty and the Boxer uprising. In 1912 he had given up journalism to become political adviser to Chiang Kai Shek, President of the recently declared Chinese Republic. Some time after his return to Peking Morrison wrote to Henry. The letter of 21 April ends as follows:

The other day I wrote to Lady May and I would like again to thank you and Lady May for the kind hospitality you showed me in Hong Kong. With great pleasure I look back to my visit. My journey round was certainly instructive and the reports I was able to make to the President have been, I hope, of some use.[62]

ST JOHN'S CATHEDRAL This is the oldest surviving Western ecclesiastical building in Hong Kong. The foundation stone was laid in 1847 and the Cathedral was completed in 1849, but underwent extension in 1873.

During the Japanese Occupation, it was converted into a club house and suffered some damage. However, it was fully repaired after the War and reopened. It was declared a monument in 1996.

However, bigger problems were looming. Phoebe was in Suffolk when war broke out in Europe at the beginning of August 1914 and she thought she might never see her family again. However, she was sustained by the news that her sister Stella had become engaged at Government House to Henry's ADC, Philip de Fonblanque. History was virtually repeating itself.[63] Eventually, Phoebe returned to Hong Kong on a P & O mail steamer in October with the Chief Justice of Hong Kong, Sir William Rees Davies, as her guardian. Her memoir ends at Mountain Lodge in mid-November 1914.

Henry stayed in post throughout the war: 'Duty with him stood first and foremost wherever his King and Country were concerned'[64] and he played his part by releasing members of the Public Service to serve at the front. A group of volunteers, known as the Hong Kong Defence Corps, were the only military unit left in Hong Kong and were actively engaged in guard and patrol duties. In addition, Henry set up the Police Reservists and endeavoured to increase the security of the colony, especially because of the potential threat from over the border. Britain also benefited from generous private donations to the war effort, such as the gift of two aeroplanes by Sir Robert Ho Tung. It was in the middle of the period of World War I that the Helena May Institute was founded – but this story will be told in the next chapter.

In 1916 Phoebe donated a side chapel to St John's Cathedral, known as the Lady Chapel. In 1956 it was moved into the former organ chamber, the present location of St Michael's Chapel, and was brought forward to its present position at the east end when the whole of the chancel layout was altered in 1968.

In his novel *Dynasty*, Robert Elegant interweaves fact and fiction. He has a description of a banquet at the Peak Hotel on 8 June 1916 with the guests arriving by sedan chair: 'The Governor's chair, marked by a gold crown, was first... Sir Francis May, tall and fiercely moustached extended a scarred hand'. (p. 277) On Saturday 17 June 1916 at Shatin '...the last race-meeting of the season... The Governor and Lady May ascended to their box, which was draped with clouds of bunting, fifteen minutes before the trumpets announced the first race'. (p. 285-6)

Farewell to Hong Kong

On 4 April 1918 Sir Robert Ho Tung's eldest daughter, Victoria, married M. K. Lo, and at the wedding the toast was given by Henry. That was probably one of his few pleasant moments that year. Scholar and historian G. R. Sayer describes it as a 'fateful year' in Hong Kong, which included a 'virtual massacre of armed robbers and police, fires in shipyards and at Happy Valley racecourse, and an outbreak of cerebro-spinal meningitis'. He goes on to say that Henry was 'breaking under the strain of seven successive summers in the Colony' and thus left on a ship for Vancouver just before news of the armistice came through.[65]

Writing in the *1918 Colonial Report*, Colonial Secretary M. Fletcher indicates that:

Sir Henry May... left the Colony in September on urgent private affairs and he subsequently resigned his appointment on grounds of health. His service under the Crown extended over 38 years and practically the whole of his career was passed in Hong Kong. He served the colony wholeheartedly with all his mind and with all his strength, and its ever increasing beauty and prosperity stand as a monument in record of his work.

During his time in Hong Kong, Henry helped to promote public works including the expansion of the Central Police Station, the Praya reclamation, the water supply reservoirs, road construction and the development of the Peak as a residential district. With his interest in sports and exercise he encouraged the development of playing fields, sea-bathing facilities and forestry paths. He is described in a handbook to the colony produced in 1920 as 'the most specially favoured of the Governors chosen for the much coveted post of Governor and Commander-in-Chief of this wonderful British Crown Colony'.[66]

Statue of Henry May

When Henry and Helena returned to England they lived at Clare Priory, which Helena inherited from her father. Henry died on 6 February 1922, aged 61, having been ill and apparently spending some time in a bathchair. In his memory a bronze statue, paid for

by public subscription, was commissioned from the eminent Australian sculptor Sir Bertram Mackennal, whose work includes the statue of Edward VII in Waterloo Place, London. This was a rare honour for anyone other than royalty, and the only statue of a governor ever erected in Statue Square. A statue of Sir Thomas Jackson of the Hong Kong & Shanghai Bank had been there since 1906, and one of an earlier governor, Sir Arthur Kennedy, had been erected in the Botanic Gardens in 1887.

Henry's statue was unveiled on 3 May 1923 by the Governor who succeeded him, Sir Reginald Stubbs. According to the report in *The Hong Kong Daily Press* the next day, there was a 'large and noteworthy gathering of residents' including 'a large number of Chinese' and 'two companies of the King's Regiment'. Sir Robert Ho Tung and Ho Fook attended, but there is no mention of their brother, Ho Kom Tong, one of the benefactors of the Helena May.

At the time of the unveiling the memorial consisted of the statue, depicting Henry sitting in a chair and wearing the official Governor's uniform, on a pedestal of polished Peterhead granite placed on a base of local granite. However, the report notes that there were plans for a much grander setting for the monument with a 28 foot granite niche including 'two ornamental piers on either side... surmounted by urns and inscribed with laurel wreaths'. Despite being ill, Henry had managed to give the sculptor 'several sittings'.

Statue Square with Henry May's statue to the left of the pier

Sir Paul Chater delivered the eulogy, having known Henry 'intimately' over almost four decades. He pointed to Henry's qualities – 'conscientiousness' and 'courage', a man 'undeterred by criticism and undaunted by obstacles', affecting people with his enthusiasm for sports, displaying 'utmost loyalty', 'abounding humour' and an 'open heart'. In his address, Stubbs noted the developments that had taken place over the time Henry had been in Hong Kong – the population had quadrupled, its shipping had trebled and the public revenue had increased fifteen times.

However, Henry has not been viewed by some historians as one of Hong Kong's most successful Governors. For instance, Frank Welsh comments in somewhat scathing terms:

When Lugard left to resume his interrupted career in Africa in March 1912, Francis May at last got the job for which – at least in his own opinion – his experience had so well qualified him. In fact it is doubtful whether May, that superb assistant, ever had possessed the qualities of a Governor. He may well have reached his level as Captain-Superintendent of Police between 1893 and 1902, when he had effected a complete reform, and a severe cull, of the force. His actions as Officer Administering the Government had often been rash and ill-considered, and he lacked the public presence which might have enabled him to face down criticism. Only to some extent were his deficiencies compensated by the qualities of his wife, the Helena May of the eponymous Institute. Almost as much a Hong Kong veteran as her husband – being the daughter of General Digby Barker, who had advocated the Kowloon extension – Helena was for 25 years at the forefront of energetic good works in the colony.[67]

Welsh goes on to point out May's 'authoritarian habits' and his inability to accept Chinese people participating in government. Nevertheless, he was revered by some people, and because of his time as President of the YMCA a portrait of him was unveiled at the building in Kowloon near the Star Ferry in 1929.

Helena's life back in Britain

After Henry's death Helena continued to live in Clare Priory. Granddaughter Lorna (daughter of Dione) remembers how she and her brother Michael stayed there 'constantly' between the ages of seven and seventeen:

She was a wonderful grandmother, and gave us a blissfully happy childhood we shall never forget. Hong Kong entered daily into the conversation and old friends from Colonial Days were frequent visitors. We were made to feel as much a part of our family's Hong Kong life as if we had experienced it ourselves. It was a very happy time.[68]

Granddaughter Mary Duncan (daughter of Stella) remembers the place as 'nearly always full of happy people... a magic place to be' partly because 'Granny always seemed to be happy, good tempered – and enjoying her life, her children and her grandchildren – and her many friends in the villages and from different parts of the world who came to stay'.[69]

Andrew Whitworth (eldest son of Phoebe) told us:

I knew my grandmother of course in the 1930s... when one of the greatest pleasures for myself, my siblings & my cousins, was to spend holidays at Clare Priory. The house was particularly suitable for grandchildren as we were able to use the billiard room as our playroom where we could make as much noise as we liked without disturbing the grown ups. The house was large enough to accommodate two or three families at the same time & my grandmother was always extremely welcoming to all visitors including children.

During the war my grandmother stayed with us for some months in Gainsborough. Great amusement was given to ourselves & our neighbours when the local grandee who lived in a big house 10 miles away, having ignored us totally, suddenly came to call, when she heard that 'Lady May' was living with us![70]

Another of Helena's 14 grandchildren, Timothy Whitworth (youngest son of Phoebe) remembers his grandmother sitting at the piano on a Sunday evening playing hymns while they all sang. One particular hymn he remembers is 'God is working his purpose out'.[71]

During World War II the Priory was used by the army as an Officers' Mess. Helena went to live with Phoebe's family in Lincolnshire and is remembered by her granddaughter, Margaret Osmaston (daughter of Phoebe), with great affection: 'She loved children and I have very happy memories of playing card games with her during long war-time evenings.'[72]

Iris and five of her children were evacuated to America from 1940 to 1943. Iris was widowed during this time and on their return to England the family moved around various rented cottages, eventually ending up in Gainsborough near the Whitworths' vicarage. Helena came to live with them once most of the children had gone off to boarding school or the army. They returned to Clare Hall in May 1944 after Uncle Gould, who had been living there, died. Youngest granddaughter Veronica Johnston (only eight at the time) remembers her Granny at this time as 'elderly, unwell and rather intimidating'. Helena died at the age of 82 on 3 October 1945. Veronica comments:

I was at Clare all the time for 3 years after Granny's death, and then at boarding school, so home in the holidays and very close to my mother... In her will the Priory was left jointly to her four daughters... There were endless problems with letting it, as it was too small for an institution but rather large for a post-war family, and it flooded in winter. My Aunt Stella was a Roman Catholic, having converted when she married Philip, and it was she who was the prime mover in offering it to the Augustinians, who were looking for a base within reach of Cambridge (for novice monks to use the University Library).[73]

1926 Helena at Clare Priory with her four eldest grandchildren. The May and Barker coats of arms are in the window. From left to right, Anne de Fonblanque, Mary de Fonblanque, Michael Kinchin Smith, Lorna Kinchin Smith

Following long negotiations and 'acts of great generosity from Lady May's heirs through which the Order acquired the property for only a fraction of its true value' the Augustinians returned to the house in 1953, and 'Stella now lies at rest in the monastic graveyard, the first Catholic to be buried there since the Reformation!'[74]

ENDNOTES

1 www.clarepriory.org.uk
2 *Who was Who 1897-1915*
3 Trollope, 1983, p.10
4 Luff, 1968, p.55
5 Bloomfield, 1984, p.8
6 *Hong Kong Hansard,* 7 December 1891, p.84
7 James, 1892
8 Whitworth, 2001, p.28-29
9 Kinchin Smith, 1992, p.16 and a letter from his wife Rachel to Mary Painter 19 April 2004
10 Lethbridge, 1970/1978, p.36-37
11 Sayer, 1975, p.111
12 Whitworth, 2001, p.9
13 Goodman, 1907, p.116-7
14 Sinclair, 1994, p.8
15 Whitworth, 2001, p.9
16 *United Empire*, March 1922
17 Sayer, 1975, p.111
18 Wiltshire, 1989, p.13
19 Crisswell & Watson, 1982, p.86
20 Unacknowledged scrapbook press-cutting supplied by Timothy Whitworth
21 Whitworth, 2001, p.140
22 Spurr, 1995, p.139
23 Wright and Cartwright, 1908
24 Quoted in Spurr, 1995, p.143
25 Whitworth, 2001, p.36, 63, 94, 120
26 Unacknowledged scrapbook press-cutting supplied by Timothy Whitworth
27 Whitworth, 2001, p.13
28 Hurley, 1920, p.78
29 Whitworth, 2001, p.18
30 Letter from Lady Meath, 25 March 1909 to the Editor of the China Mail
31 Welsh, 1993, p.342
32 Lethbridge, quoted in Welsh, 1993, p.342
33 Whitworth, 2001, p.21
34 http://centenary.scmp.com/cenarts/mp1903/zzzj06wbnmd.html
35 Welsh, 1993, p.343
36 Hoe, 1991, p.202
37 Endacott, 1964, p.284
38 Courtauld, 1997, p.42
39 Bloomfield, 1984, p.88-89
40 Trollope, 1983, p.173
41 Perham, 1960, p.286
42 Mellor,1992, p.16
43 Perham, 1960, p. 289-291
44 Trollope, 1983, p.185
45 Crisswell & Watson, 1982, p.100
46 Scrapbook press-cutting supplied by Timothy Whitworth
47 Unacknowledged scrapbook press-cutting supplied by Timothy Whitworth
48 Whitworth, 2001, p.70
49 Whitworth, 2001, p.74
50 Whitworth, 2001, p.75
51 Unacknowledged scrapbook press-cutting supplied by Timothy Whitworth
52 Airlie, 1989, p.163
53 Whitworth, 2001, p.127
54 Jarrett, 1935
55 Bloomfield, 1984, p.89
56 Spurr, 1995, p.137
57 Morrison, 1978
58 Mellor, 1980, Vol. I p.22, 23, 26, 59
59 http://centenary.scmp.com/cenarts/mp1913/zzzrg0jmwkd.html
60 http://centenary.scmp.com/cenarts/mp1913/zzz0kajmwkd.html
61 Administrative Report 1913, p.16-17
62 Morrison, 1978, p.309-311
63 Letter from Mary Duncan to Mary Painter, May 2004
64 Hurley, 1920, p.79
65 Sayer, 1975, p.122
66 Hurley, 1920, p.77
67 Welsh, 1993, p.359
68 Relayed from Lorna Headlam-Morley in a letter from her son Peter and daughter-in law Alexandra to Mary Painter, September 2005
69 Letter from Mary Duncan to Mary Painter, May 2004
70 Letter from Andrew Whitworth to Mary Painter, December 2004
71 Private communication to Mary Painter, June 2004
72 Letter from Margaret Osmaston to Mary Painter, April 2004
73 Private communication to Esther Morris, January 2006
74 http://www.davidsemporium.co.uk/st.marys/clare.html

Hong Kong Docks.

Mrs Cooke Miss Barker Adamson (crew) Mr Cooke Mrs May Geo: Barker

Baddeley (crew) May (Skipper) Gedge (crew)

Launch of the Stella. Season 93/4

Tomtit   Tai   Mr. & Mrs. May.

Digby   Helena Barker   Carrie Barker   May Gresson

1891

2. *Pioneering Colonial Women and the Birth of the Helena May*

PIONEERING WOMEN

As the nineteenth century progressed in Britain, and despite Queen Victoria's inclinations, women expanded their horizons. There were icons like Florence Nightingale, who reformed army nursing in 1855 by introducing hygiene into hospitals during the Crimean War, and the less well-known, but equally impressive Jamaican healer, Mary Seacole, who saved many soldiers' lives. Together they highlighted the great contribution that nurses could make in building the Empire. A few years later Elizabeth Blackwell in America and Elizabeth Garrett in Britain were showing that it was not only men who could be doctors.

Also in 1855 in London, Emma Robarts and Mary Jane Kinnaird founded separate Young Women's Christian Associations (YWCA). They were pioneers who believed that women should help other women.[1] A network of groups was formed across Britain to help young women with accommodation, education and healthcare. By 1890 the movement had reached China and the first group was established by an American missionary for students in Hangzhou.

It was very difficult for women to obtain a university education at this time, but two leaders of the feminist movement, Emily Davies and Barbara Bodichon, began raising money and the first residential college for women, Girton, was established in 1869 in Cambridge, England. Before Helena Barker left Britain in 1890, the technology of the telephone and the typewriter had opened the way for work in jobs that required the female characteristics of 'nimble fingers, patience and a polite manner'.[2] Increasingly there were pioneers in various fields, thus changing the status of women.

In London and other big cities some women began to move around freely on their own, becoming bolder in their dress and their manner – smoking, riding bicycles, playing tennis, controlling their own finances, attending colleges and challenging men. Meanwhile other women were redirecting their emotional talents and becoming missionaries of different sorts. As well as the regular parish work for the better off, there were campaigns against slavery, poverty and prostitution. Middle class intellectuals petitioned for birth control and the right to vote, whereas working girls supported the trade union movement to fight enthusiastically for better pay and conditions.

The more intrepid ventured overseas. While the wealthy were able to follow their passions for natural history, geology, art, anthropology and culture in Europe and the Middle East, the less wealthy, especially those in the 20 to 30 age range, emigrated – helped along by male migration to the colonies and the

British Women's Emigration Association advertising the opportunities available 'to civilize the world and secure British values in the colonies'.[3] Some settled in Australia and North America and swapped the harsh realities of industrialized Britain for the promise of riches to come in newer lands. Others saw the opportunities that the British Empire in Africa and Asia afforded them – to convert 'heathen souls', find employment or a husband, or just experience other cultures.

Another group of women who went to the colonies have been described as 'the helpmates of administrators and the meliorators of the worst manifestations of indigenous and colonial oppression.'[4] Some coped by throwing themselves into home-making and childrearing, while others intellectualized the situation and became more involved in the work their husbands were undertaking. Thus some colonial wives were much more than companions for their husbands, mothers of the next generation, supervisors of the home and servants, adornments at official functions and providers of hospitality for visitors and new arrivals. 'They were representatives of the home culture, and of its moral standards.'[5] They had a stabilizing and civilizing influence on colonial society. Although their lives often revolved around social gatherings, they also provided a readily available reserve pool of labour and a good deal of productive charity work was being done that 'contributed to supporting the empire.'[6] Indeed, colonial wives have been described as 'one of the empire's greatest assets'.[7]

Western Women in Hong Kong

Fortunately there were ladies who kept diaries and wrote to friends and relatives back home. And there were people who managed to preserve these documents so that we can glean many interesting details about their lives. Thus we know that some of these women wanted to enjoy the same activities as their husbands – be it amateur dramatics or tennis. Those who began to feel the need for a place to exercise requested land for the purpose, and although some government administrators apparently thought this a bit of a joke, the Ladies Recreation Club was founded in 1883 and eventually opened the following year.[8]

Nurses were desperately needed as the mortality rate amongst even upper class Europeans was a 'frightening feature'.[9] Judge William Goodman, who later came to Helena and Henry's wedding, became a widower when his wife died suddenly of dysentery in May 1890, and the wife of Governor Robinson died of an undiagnosed tropical disease in 1894 – the year bubonic plague battered Hong Kong. The Colonial Nursing Association, based in London was established in 1896 by Mabel Piggott, who came to Hong Kong when her husband was appointed Chief Justice in 1905. Meanwhile in March 1902, following his mother's wishes, Edward VII announced the establishment of Queen Alexandra's Imperial Military Nursing Service: 'The seal of high social approval rested firmly upon the profession at last.'[10]

There was an abundance of benevolent ladies' committees set up in the late nineteenth and early twentieth centuries to help the community. In 1903 the Hong Kong branch of the Ministering Children's League raised $1,000 through a sale, which was presented by Helena and Henry May to the Hildesheim Home for blind Chinese girls. Helena, as wife of the then Colonial Secretary, was patroness of the Hong Kong Nursing Institution (which had been set up in 1901) while Mabel, later Lady, Piggott served on the committee and eventually helped it out of its financial and organizational difficulties.

The wives of colonial men performed other functions as well, and so on 30 July 1904, Mrs Jones, whose husband was the Director of Public Works, had the privilege of driving the first single-deck, yellow and chocolate coloured tramcar from the Causeway Bay depot. Helena had many duties to perform and few would have been this exciting. An article on the history of Hong Kong appearing in the *South China Morning Post* as part of a series by 'Colonial' notes that Lady May was one of the guests at the 1910 Golden Jubilee of the Canossian Convent on Caine Road, where 'the programme was very interesting but somewhat long.'[11]

Meanwhile there were also the single ladies who came to Hong Kong of their own accord. Of particular relevance to this history is Lucy Eyre, who arrived from Britain in 1889 as one of a band of missionaries attached to the Female Education Society (FES).[12] She joined the mission at Fairlee, a centre for women's work and a school, which was the forerunner of the Diocesan Girls' School (founded in 1899 and where Helena served on the committee[13]), St Stephen's Girls' College (which Helena was also associated with, as we shall see later) and Heep Yunn School – the alma maters of many Chinese women who have also played important roles in Hong Kong. All of these institutions were controlled by the Church Missionary Society (CMS).

Lucy particularly wished to help Eurasian girls and also set up the Hong Kong Refuge for Chinese Women and Girls in Pokfulam. This rivalled the refuge set up by the Chinese – the Po Leung Kuk – which Lucy viewed as a 'heathen' place.[14] However, a more important difference was that the latter only took girls up to the age of 18.

Agnes Hamper, an honorary CMS missionary, took over the running of the Victoria Home and Orphanage in 1892. This institution, which had been set up in 1881 to care for 'rescued "slaves" and Chinese and Eurasian orphans', was helped by Helena, her daughters and the Ministering Children's League.[15]

(In 1937 the orphanage was closed and the girls were transferred to the CMS Heep Yunn School.)

From 1893 Lucy and Agnes started meetings with Chinese Christian women, and this later became the Young Women's Christian Association (YWCA) of Hong Kong. This organization has been credited with introducing Asian women to new ideas, principles and customs – bringing them out of the home and expanding their horizons.[16] Its object was 'to provide for the general welfare of young women in the Colony' and, despite the name, the membership was 'undenominational'. It was managed by a council of ladies with committees for religious, social and educational work, although the emphasis was definitely on the religious aspect.

In 1906, whilst the women's suffrage movement was becoming more active in Britain, two good things happened for females in Hong Kong. Firstly, the Married Women's Property Ordinance was passed. Reflecting the cultural lag so typical in the colony, it came much later than in Britain, where an equivalent law had been in force since 1882.

Secondly, St Stephen's Girls College was opened in Caine Road (it moved to its current location in Lyttelton Road in 1923), building on its forerunner, St Stephen's Preparatory School, which had started the previous year. The first Principal was a Miss Carden of the CMS, who was a Cantonese speaker and appreciated the resistance amongst upper-class Chinese to having their daughters educated outside the home.[17] The Mays seem to have had considerable contact with the school – probably because it was serving the elite families of the colony, such as the Ho Tungs. Also, the Anglican Bishop of Hong Kong and much of the clergy were from the CMS and there were close relationships between Government House, the Church of England and the political and religious foundations of Hong Kong society.

Helena attended a presentation ceremony when Miss Carden left for an extended leave on 13 July 1910. She had also entertained members of the college the previous day at Mountain Lodge. One of the teachers at St Stephen's, Miss Griffin, had served as a governess to the May daughters. She was very keen on sporting activities and so 'on certain days of the week senior pupils were invited (by Lady May) to play tennis, sometimes with her daughters, at Mountain Lodge'.[18] Helena helped the school, through Henry as

Students and teachers with Lady May at Mountain Lodge around 1912

Governor, to acquire land for expansion in 1913.[19] When Miss Griffin conducted her first prize-giving as Principal in 1916 it was Helena who distributed the awards.

In January 1907 another pioneering lady, Matilda Lincolne, was honoured. The Matilda Hospital opened its doors to patients at that time, having been named by businessman Granville Sharp in loving memory of his wife, who died in 1893 and is reputed to have been the first person to be cremated in Hong Kong.[20] They had arrived newly married in Hong Kong in 1858, and Matilda later joined the first tour group to Europe organised by Thomas Cook, who established business in London in 1865. As a former schoolteacher but childless herself, Matilda became interested in the education of Chinese girls and learnt Cantonese.[21] She did a lot of work for widows and orphans, and no doubt therefore Helena would have known her through the Hong Kong Benevolent Society (HKBS). This body was founded in 1889 as a charity comprising 'a committee of bountiful ladies' to formalise welfare for expatriates. Thus Matilda became affectionately known in both the Western and Chinese communities.[22] Ironically her husband's detailed bequest included a 'no Chinese' clause – perhaps going against the lady's own sentiments.

One colonial lady mentioned in the first chapter, and possibly a role model for Helena, was the quite remarkable Flora Shaw, wife of Governor Lord Lugard. Born in 1852, she started to travel abroad in her twenties and became a novelist. It has been said that few late-nineteenth century writers have had more influence on colonial affairs.[23] She worked hard to convince the editor of *The Times* that more should be published about the colonies and eventually became the leading writer on imperial affairs. She was a mature woman at the height of her career when she met Lugard, an army officer seven years younger, in West Africa. They married in 1902, and subsequently she spent her life devoted to his career. She was a driving force behind the creation of the University of Hong Kong through her friendship with Parsee businessman Hormusjee Navrotjee Mody, who funded the project. Flora's diary for the first few weeks of her stay in Hong Kong from 1907 shows that she was approached by Lucy Eyre for help with funding the Hong Kong refuge, and also made visits to the various other institutions mentioned above.

While on a visit to Hong Kong in 1909, Lady Meath sent a letter dated 25 March from Government House to the Editor of the *China Mail* to report on 'a gathering of young folks belonging to the Ministering Children's League' at the garden of the Bishop of Hong Kong's residence. Helena, 'the popular and energetic wife of the Colonial Secretary', is credited with introducing this world wide undenominational league to Hong Kong and raising money for the charities it supported. Lady Meath describes its object as being 'to train young people in unselfish ways and especially to teach them how to be of service to those who suffer.' The League was introduced to the girls at St Stephen's, with the idea of extending their good deeds into China.

A seed is sown and an institution is born

The institution that Lucy Eyre and Agnes Hamper founded in 1893, and that became known as the YWCA, is shrouded in mystery. According to research done by Susanna Hoe: 'By 1896 Lucy was writing of a European committee and the need to help Eurasian girls. But it was not until 1909 that the organization managed to find a home, in Beaconsfield Arcade.'[24] This splendid building, on the site opposite the current location of the HSBC head office in Queen's Road Central, was demolished long ago, but at that time it was '...where Bible Classes and needle work classes were held and where members had an opportunity of reading periodicals or of enjoying the society of one another'.[25]

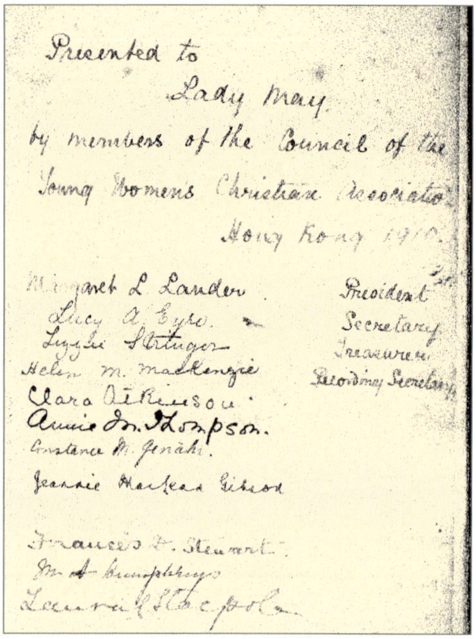
Presented to
Lady May
by members of the Council of the
Young Womens Christian Association
Hong Kong 1910.

Margaret L Lander — President
Lucy A. Eyre — Secretary
Lizzie Stringer — Treasurer
Helen M. Mackenzie — Recording Secretary
Clara Atkinson
Annie M. Thompson
Constance M. Jenahi
Jeannie Maclean Gibson

Frances F. Stewart
M. A. Humphreys
[illegible]

A bible was presented to Helena before the family left for Fiji in January 1911 and in it are inscribed the signatures of some of the members of the YWCA, including Margaret L. Lander (wife of the Bishop) as president and Lucy Eyre as secretary. Helena's interest in the institution possibly stemmed from the fact that her godmother, Princess Helena, was a patron of the YWCA in Britain.

In his speech at the opening in 1916[26] Henry gave some of the background that links the demise of Lucy Eyre's YWCA to the foundation of the Helena May:

In 1912 this room (in Beaconsfield Arcade) was closed and for a time the Association was homeless. Later in that year part of the top floor of Beaconsfield was secured, but before the end of the year that was lost as the whole of the house fell into the hands of one owner. The Association then found refuge in the rooms of Mr H. E. Pollock, K. C. who during his absence from the Colony kindly placed his room at their disposal, and in September, 1913, the Association sought refuge in two rooms in Queen's Road.

Having to close for the summer months 'was to prove how absolutely necessary a suitable and convenient room is to the work of the Society.'[27] Sadly, Lucy Eyre died from a relapse of malaria on 22 September 1912. Her loss was deeply felt, and in the report the Council expressed their 'deep appreciation of the excellent work she did for so many years among young women in the Colony'.[28] The report ends by noting:

It was Miss Eyre's great desire to see in Hong Kong some sort of lodging accommodation under the auspices of the YWCA for women passing through en route to other places, as well as for residents needing temporary

---

Inscription in presentation bible

shelter. The Council are fully in sympathy with the idea because they know the need is a real one. The past year alone has given instances of this. At present sufficient funds are lacking but it is hoped that in the near future the necessary money may be forthcoming and that ladies travelling alone may find in Hong Kong something of the same kind of lodging as is provided for them in Colombo, Singapore, Bombay, Calcutta and Shanghai, and for which we are constantly being asked.[29]

Young Women's Christian Association.

HONGKONG.

President—Lady May.

1912.

Printed by Wing Fat & Co, Hongkong.

The object of the Hong Kong YWCA, according to its report of 1912, was 'to provide for the general welfare of young women in the Colony'[30] and Helena, as the mother of four daughters, was probably aware of the lack of facilities for women and girls in Hong Kong. At the time there were 112 YWCA members, of whom 40 were young and earning their living as nurses, teachers, typists and shop assistants. A further 20 were also young, some married and some not, but they were not earning their own living. There was a category described as 'sustaining members' who were 'of riper years and wider experience' and 24 of these ladies served on the committees and were the backbone of the 'Society'. The social side of the organization involved bathing parties and tennis. There were lectures on 'home nursing', drawing, singing and French, and the Education Committee arranged for a lecture on a stated subject to be given daily in ten week courses. Religious work involved Bible classes on Tuesdays and Sundays. There was also a reading club and a 'Miss May' was one of the librarians. This would almost certainly have been Stella: 'rising 20, lively and energetic and needing constructive occupation'.[31] There is also mention[32] of the National YWCA Secretary for China, Miss Paddock, conducting a prayer meeting – so there were links.

Following the collapse of the Qing Dynasty and the establishment of the Republic of China in October 1911, Hong Kong experienced a massive influx of refugees and, according to one contemporary account, the city was 'packed full of ruffians and robbers who have come down from Canton...'.[33] Thus, new arrivals needed safe and well-managed accommodation.

During the period leading up to World War I women began to be considered as individuals rather than as mere appendages of their husbands and families. By 1913 the issue of votes for women was being debated in Parliament in Britain and increasing numbers of women were entering the workforce at a professional and semi-professional level. These trends were reflected in the number of women arriving in Hong Kong seeking employment. The city offered few facilities for non-Chinese, many of whom, like Lucy Eyre, were single missionaries who had been transferred south or who were based in China but were required to visit Hong Kong regularly.

YWCA report 1912 with Helena's name on cover

The need for a women's hostel was emphasised at the Annual Meeting of the HKBS held in January 1913 and it was suggested that the YWCA would be the most appropriate body to manage such a place. Bishop Lander, the Bishop of Victoria, commented at the Meeting that he was asked constantly to name an institution where women coming to the Colony could stay and was ashamed when he had to reply that there was no such hostel in the city. Hong Kong boasted numerous hotels but many were of dubious reputation and the more respectable were beyond the means of the average working woman. The Government provided quarters for the nurses and teachers in its employ but similar provision was rarely made for women working in the private sector.

Susanna Hoe thinks that 'it was probably at this time that the Chinese side of the YWCA went, as it were, underground, in some girl schools, later to re-emerge'.[34] According to the official history,[35] the Hong Kong Chinese YWCA was inaugurated on 10 March 1920. The wife of the Colonial Secretary in 1921, Nan Severn, wrote in letters home that the YWCA for expatriates in Hong Kong had been 'replaced'.[36] The English Speaking Members Department of the Hong Kong YWCA did not open until 1945. Meanwhile Lucy Eyre's YWCA and the HKBS merged, and a scheme was initiated with the object of establishing a Women's Institute. For this purpose $11,611 had been collected by the end of 1913.[37]

'Almost as a New Year gift'[38] on 22 January of 1914, Helena received a letter from a prominent Hong Kong businessman and philanthropist, Mr (later Sir) Ellis Kadoorie, via his solicitors. (The 1934 history seems to have some mistakes and records his name as 'Mr Elly Kadoorie'. It also has 'Mr Ho Kam Tong' instead of Mr Ho Kom Tong, and the opening date as 16 September instead of 12 September. We cannot be sure therefore of all the 'facts' given.) In the letter Mr Kadoorie offered:

...the sum of $15,000 for the purpose of erecting a Hostel or Women's Institute in the Colony, provided that a similar sum could be raised within two years. This money, he stipulated, was a free gift to Lady May to be used as she desired, with the single proviso that any institution so formed should bear her name.[39]

Upon receiving the letter, Lady May called a meeting of the YWCA/HKBS, and it was unanimously decided that this scheme could have much wider scope than under the Association; that the offer should therefore be most gratefully accepted; and that the funds already collected towards the erection of the new building should be transferred.[40] In accepting the offer Helena wrote:

I have for some years past been closely associated with the work of the YWCA and I have no doubt it was the knowledge that this association has no building of its own and is hampered by want of funds that prompted your kind offer... It is our intention that the YWCA shall merge in due course into the new Institute, which will be managed on similar lines, and, if your generosity meets with response from others, with a much wider scope.[41]

She somewhat reluctantly agreed to the condition concerning the name, saying that she preferred 'The Helena May Institute for Women'. Mr Kadoorie's letter and her reply were then forwarded to the local newspapers in order to encourage others to contribute to the fund. Following formal acceptance of the offer the name of the Association was changed to The Hong Kong Women's Institute.

On 30 January 1914, Mr Ho Kom Tong offered to pay the other half of the cost.

Mrs Edkins, who had been appointed first honorary secretary to Council, thereupon wrote to Miss Coppock, Secretary of the YWCA National Committee in Shanghai, telling her of the proposed change – 'we trust and believe the Institute will be a centre of great blessing and usefulness in the Colony' – asking for formal recognition and requesting that the money already raised by the YWCA, the Mothers' Union, and the Benevolent Society, might be made over to this object. After a National Committee Meeting, Miss Coppock wrote on February 21st, 1914, expressing complete sympathy and concurrence, but adding that 'we of course do not consider that the above plan affects the Chinese women of Hong Kong. When there is need for our type of work for Chinese women, we shall expect that to be done under the YWCA.' ...A letter to this effect was also sent to the World's YWCA in London. So, bearing in mind the aims of the YWCA, the need for both social and religious welfare work among women living in the colony, and the above stipulations, the original Constitution was drawn up.[42]

No time was lost in selecting a suitable site for the building. In a memorandum to the Director of Public Works which bears the same date as Mr Kadoorie's letter to Lady May, the Governor asked if a site could be suggested 'on Crown Land as near as possible to the Lower Tram Station'. The Governor commented that the building would not be large, 'not larger than a commodious house of say eight or nine rooms'. Various sites were suggested including one in Wyndham Street and another at the junction of Kennedy and Garden Roads above St Joseph's Church. Governor May was not satisfied with these suggestions and pressed for a site below (i.e. north) of the church. One can imagine the Mays discussing the site over dinner with Lady May emphasising the need for a convenient location within easy walking distance of the city and perhaps specifying that it be close to Government House and the Cathedral. The wishes of Colonial Governors were seldom ignored by their subordinates and the site preferred by Sir Henry May was approved, granted and leased for seventy-five years at a crown rent of $50 per annum. Messrs Denison, Ram and Gibbs were appointed the architects and plans were drawn up for an 'adapted Renaissance style' building comprising an office, reading room, dining room, lounge, two classrooms, a small library and matron's quarters. The upper storey was to accommodate eight bedrooms with the provision for four more if required.[43]

According to the 1934 version of the history of the Helena May, the site was purchased for £3,600, the architect's plans were accepted and Mr Kadoorie signed the building contract '...thus making himself personally responsible, and further agreed to pay for furniture, provided that the total commitments did not exceed $35,000.'[44] Construction commenced in 1914 on Inland Lot 2083 Garden Road. Other buildings in progress that year were new premises for the Sincere Company in Wing Wo Street, a new church and school in connection with the Rhenish Mission on Bonham Road, and maternity wards at the Matilda Hospital on Mount Kellett Road.[45]

Fund-raising continued throughout 1914 and noted contributors were Mr Chan Kai Ming and Mr Lau Chu Pak, who donated $3,000 each. Mrs M. Kemp, Honorary Treasurer of the fund, acknowledged all donations including one for $10 from Miss May. Sir Ellis Kadoorie eventually contributed $62,000 which, apart from helping to pay for the building, defrayed the cost of covering the Albany Nullah which ran beside the site, the laying out of a garden and internal furnishings.

At the opening of the Helena May, Henry noted with regard to the YWCA that:

The rooms in Queen's Road were given up in May of the same year (1914) as being too hot in the summer months and in October rooms were rented at Cragcliffe, Pedder's Hill. In June 1915 these rooms were given up and in August rooms were obtained rent free for a short time in Beaconsfield. These were vacated in October of the same year and since that date the Institute has had no habitation of it own... The frequent change of headquarters shows to what vicissitudes the Association and Institute have been subjected and proves the necessity for a fixed permanent abode.[46]

MEANWHILE... The editor of the *South China Morning Post*[47] was worried about 'picture palaces' and their influence on children. The relationship between 'attendance at the cinematograph and crime is well established' he wrote. 'The lurid melodrama which pictures revenge and murder is responsible for much that cause the young mind to stray.'

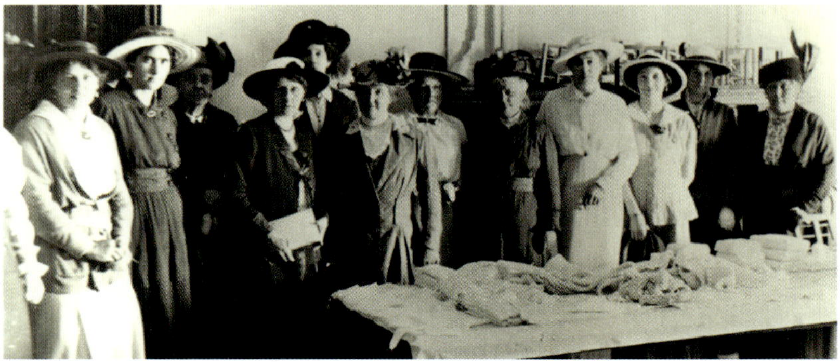

Hong Kong residents were asked by a writer with the pseudonym 'The Jat' to write to the Home Secretary in London about suffragettes and their 'enormous wilful damage'. He advised 'horrified and disgusted Hongkongers' to write to the 'weak-kneed govern-

Helena and other ladies packing bandages

ment and invertebrate Home Secretary to establish immediately a corps of Amazon police to act against suffragettes'. 'The Jat' wanted Hong Kong citizens to express a desire to birch women who demanded the vote, and to put them in prison garb and on prison rations. It would be interesting to know whether there was any support for such an idea. Perhaps the Women's Institute, which was founded in Britain in 1915, seemed less threatening – though in recent times its members have also shown themselves to be political.

Women were definitely spreading their wings, and one intended function of the Helena May Institute was to provide accommodation for those who were travelling the world. It is interesting therefore to read a first-hand account of the impression Hong Kong made on a young woman arriving for the first time. Mary Poynter's travel diary was published in 1921 and the book may well have found its way into the library at the Institute.

As the 'Great War' started to rage in Europe in August Hong Kong was fortunate to be in the relatively peaceful Pacific region, but played its part in the war effort by building ships, servicing those that came into its harbour, and raising funds. The expatriate ladies of the colony – in particular the 'big' ladies, who were the wives of the seven senior colonial position holders – played their part through various charities. Helena was unusual for a Governor's wife in that she had already lived in Hong Kong for some time and combined 'commitment to the local community' with a love of the place. She willingly took the lead that was expected of her:

Hong Kong was far away from the centre of action but its women raised money and produced clothes... Helena was often a link between organizations in Hong Kong and Britain.[48]

Society life in Hong Kong continued, however, and according to the Ladies' Column in the *Post* in 1914: 'fur trim on a chiffon evening dress was a sartorial must' which should 'ideally be arranged against the bodice to emphasise the whiteness and delicacy of the skin'. The department store of Whiteaway Laidlaw on Des Voeux Road, Central, had held a special exhibition of the famous 'W. B.' corsets. An expert and fitter were present to assist ladies in their choice of undergarments. Starting at $2.50, corsets were meant to shape and mould a woman's figure, reducing hip measurements by up to 12 centimetres. Attendance at the store was considerable.[49]

In 1915, the Women's Institute was founded in Britain and Robert Ho Tung was knighted. The following year the first company of Girl Guides was formed in Hong Kong's Victoria British School and the Helena May building was completed.

FIRST IMPRESSIONS OF HONG KONG: 1914 We were in a way unprepared for and most pleasantly surprised with Hong Kong as seen from the sea and with the island-encircled, far-spreading harbour as seen from the land. It seems as if this fair port has a right to feel aggrieved that its praises have not been more widely sung... Its typhoons alone seem to be widely advertised... (yet) Hong-Kong island sits for the most part in placid majesty and an even, damp temperature throughout the year. Whether you sail in by day or by night, it has a compelling attraction. By day its abrupt, almost perpendicular green heights, with embowered houses nestling here and there, almost to the very summit of the Peak, with the city itself, Victoria by name (though seldom called by its rightful appellation) at its base in the foreground make immediate appeal. At night, with the thousands of ships' lights in the harbour, with the city's own illumination and the twinkling lights all along the peak that make it difficult when looking up to tell where the stars on land leave off and those in the sky begin, it appeals perhaps still more.

And if you go east or west, go always you must to Hong Kong, for it is a port that lies ever in your path, not obtrusively, but as a calling-place on your way to 'somewhere else'. Though it is British soil, which I believe the traveller finds the most international soil on earth, one feels that the great mysterious Chinese Empire – no, Republic at the moment – lies just beyond, though never assertive to the outer world, struggling within itself, struggling to keep body and soul together, the individual always working, working at home if there be room for him and working in every land outside that will open its doors to him.

You may stay only a day or a whole week at Hong Kong, but your first pilgrimage on the island will be made to the Peak, either on foot or by cable railway... and generous is the hospitality throughout all the East...

The sedan chair is the most popular vehicle in Hong Kong, though 'rickishas [sic] and even occasional motor-cars are in evidence where there are level roads... There is a sharp line, shall I say of cleanliness, drawn between the native Chinese and the English part of the city, and Europeans only are allowed to occupy houses on the Peak.

...ships call and pass on north, south and eastward as they please from this port that was built on a rock to accommodate the traffic of the sea. Thus today, Hong Kong, "good harbour", that a little over seventy years ago was a waste place, a haunt of pirates in fact, is a free port, second in importance as a shipping centre to none in the world.

Mary Poynter (1921, p.149) arriving by ship on 28 March 1914

South China Morning Post

Wednesday, September 13, 1916

The Helena May Institute

FORMALLY OPENED BY H. E. THE GOVERNOR

The Helena May Institute, which forms a splendid addition to Hong Kong s many imposing buildings, was formally opened yesterday by His Excellency the Governor, Sir F. H. May, K.C.M.G.

Prior to the opening a large company had assembled. Among those noticed being present were the following, H. E. the Governor, Lady May and the Misses May, the Hon. Mr Claud Severn (Colonial Secretary), Hon. Mr J. H. Kemp (Attorney General), Sir Robert and Lady Ho Tung, Sir William and Lady Rees Davies, Hon. Mr E. Shellim, Hon. Mr H. E. Pollock, K.C., Bishop of Victoria (Dr. Lander), Mr Ellis Kadoorie, Mr Ho Kom Tong, Rev. V. H. Copley Moyle, Rev. No. C. Pope, Mr T. H. King, Mr Kraft, Mr E Ralphs.

The Members of the Council of the Institute and a large company of other ladies were also present.

On the arrival of His Excellency the ceremony of opening was commenced by a speech by Mr Ho Kom Tong who said:

Your Excellency, Lady May, Ladies and Gentlemen. It is a pleasure as well as an honour to me to be the spokesman on this occasion on behalf of Mr Kadoorie and the others of us who have made ourselves responsible for the purchase of this site and the erection, furnishing and part endowment of this building.

It is only fair to say at once that the brunt of the burden has been shouldered by Mr Kadoorie, who has from the beginning devoted himself heart and soul to the completion of the project, and he therefore deserves the lion s share of the credit. (Applause)

Now let me explain what the project is and how it originated. Early in 1914 the gracious lady whose name this Institute is to bear, Lady May, interested herself in the movement for the foundation of a Hostel for women the need for which had long been felt, and Mr Kadoorie of his own initiative made his first generous offer which brought the scheme at once within the range of practical politics, stipulating only that if the funds required were secured and a building were erected it should be called after Lady May. (Applause) *He felt, as we all feel, that in asking her to allow her name to be associated with the Institute the honour was hers not to receive but to bestow.* (Applause)

In fact we are all glad that an opportunity has been thus afforded of bringing into existence some tangible and permanent manifestation of the high esteem and affectionate regard in which her Ladyship is held in this colony, (Applause) *and I venture to think that this handsome building upon the portal of which her name is to remain in perpetuity bids fair to be emblematic of her all embracing sympathy and kindly concern for the welfare of every one with whom she is brought in contact.* (Applause)

In its inception no doubt the paramount idea was to provide Headquarters for working women either resident in or passing through the Colony on the lines of similar places to be found in Colombo, Singapore and elsewhere in the East. But as the scheme took shape and this site was found it became clear that something rather more ambitious and at the same time more comprehensive in its scope might with advantage be undertaken an Institute that would offer to all alike opportunities of social intercourse, mutual helpfulness, improvement and recreation.

I believe all formalities in connection with the legal transfer of the site and building to the Incorporated Body which has been formed under the name of the Helena May Institute for Women, with Lady May as the first President, have already been completed. The furnishing and equipment of the building have been considerably delayed by the difficulties of obtaining various articles from England under present conditions of shipping but to all intents and purposes the Institute is now complete and ready for the purpose for which it is intended. It is a great pleasure to all of us who have been associated in its promotion to see the result of our efforts so satisfactorily attained, a result for which we owe a special debt of gratitude to our Architect, Mr Ram, and I now leave it to Mr Kadoorie, to whom this special privilege undoubtedly belongs, to make the formal presentation of the key of the building to His Excellency Sir Henry May whom it is our delight to honour. (Applause)

In handing His Excellency the key of the door Mr Ellis Kadoorie said:

Your Excellency, I am proud to have the privilege of handing you this key, with which I ask Your Excellency to be graciously pleased to open this Institute, which I trust will realize all the anticipations formed with regard to it. I beg that Your Excellency will keep the key as a souvenir of this occasion. (Applause)

The key presented was of an appropriate design and was attached to a knot of purple ribbon. H. E. the Governor:

Thank you very much. With a view to avoiding domestic trouble I will ask Lady May to unlock the door. (Laughter)

Lady May then opened the double doors and company entered the building, where in the large hall further speeches were made. On the platform His Excellency was supported by Dr Lander, Mr Ellis Kadoorie and Mr Ho Kom Tong. Addressing those present His Excellency said:

My Lord Bishop, ladies and gentlemen. The Institute which "by my kind permission Lady May has just opened has its origin in the Young Women s Christian Association inaugurated so far back as the year 1898 by the late Miss Eyre, a name familiar to us in Hong Kong in connection with much good work for the benefit of women.

* * * * *

The cutlery and crockery has not yet arrived, for as you know there is difficulty in obtaining such articles from Home. He (Mr Kadoorie) has also presented the Institute with a portrait of Lady May from the brush of a very competent Italian artist Mr. Belsito, whom most of you will know. For these munificent gifts we owe our heart-felt gratitude. For the building fund Mr Ho Kom Tong has given the handsome sum of $25,000 and Mr Chan Kai Ming and Mr Lau Chu Pak have given $3,000 each (Applause), *while $15,250 has been raised by gifts from 97 donors for an endowment fund including $2,000 each from Sir Robert Ho Tung, Mr Ho Kom Tong and Mr Lau Chu Pak and $1,000 from Mr Ivor Gourgey.* (Applause)

The beautiful building which you find yourselves in today is well adapted to supply wants which have long been felt in this Colony. In the first place we have at present eight bedrooms available for women who are earning their living in this Colony and for friendless women who may be passing through it, and we can provide 4 more bedrooms if there is demand for them. The rooms will be allotted by a Sub Committee and care will be taken that the hospitality of the Institute is not abused. Occupants can board in the Institute and it is hoped that with this convenience there will be a steady demand for rooms on the letting of which the financial success of the Institute will in no small measure depend. The Building comprises an office, reading room, dining room, lounge, two class rooms, small library, and Matron's quarters. The constitution of the Institute provides ample scope for the religious and secular work of the women of Hong Kong.

As its centre and pivot there will be its religious life open to all but thrust upon none. A feature of the Institution will be its educational side under the charge of a Sub Committee whose function it will be to arrange lectures and courses of study for which there may seem to be a demand amongst members. There will be a Social Committee whose duty it will be to arrange concerts and other social entertainments and there will of course be the usual Sub Committees to look after the internal economy of the Institute. The Institute has a small endowment fund mentioned above. It is largely dependent therefore on its membership fees and on the rental it obtains for its rooms. A strong membership is therefore an urgent necessity and I appeal to all women eligible for membership to join this Institute and to give it their help financially and otherwise.

Ladies and Gentlemen, the war has shown in a remarkable manner what splendid work women can do in directions hitherto closed to their energies. When peace is restored we may look to see women taking a far greater share in our national life than has hitherto been their opportunity. It seems opportune therefore at this juncture that this Institute should be opened when it can fittingly and usefully form the centre of women s work in this Colony. I would like to add a word or two of advice and encouragement. The management of this Institute is the largest work which women have undertaken as yet in this Colony. The task in this mixed community will not be an easy one. Your financial problem will not be the least of your difficulties. You may find yourselves exposed to plenty of criticism especially from people who will not have sufficient knowledge to criticise usefully. I shall watch your work with an interest enhanced by the fact that honour has been done Lady May in calling the Institute by her name. And I am convinced that by the exercise of thrift, patience and unselfishness, characteristics which mark women far above men, your success is well assured. **(Applause)**

In conclusion I would like to record the useful and hard work done by the ladies of the Council and especially by the two Secretaries of this Institute (Applause).

Dr Lander then read the following dedicatory prayer:

Almighty God Vouchsafe we beseech Thee Thy divine blessing upon this building. Grant that whatever's done there may be for Thy glory and the good of Thy people in body and soul. May those who teach be themselves first taught of Thee. May those who pray here do so by the inspiration of Thy spirit. May all who sojourn here be kept in Thy peace. May those who eat and drink here remember Thee the Giver of all. May those who hold converse manifest the spirit of charity and love. Within these walls may harsh thoughts be ever subdued and unkind words unspoken. Grant that all who enter this Institute may be drawn towards whatsoever is of good report, so that there may emanate from hence an ever extending influence making for high ideals and holy lives till we all attain to everlasting life through Jesus Christ our Lord.

The Doxology brought the ceremony to a close. Refreshments were served in the grounds, the band of the Hong Kong Police Regiment rendering choice selections.

DESCRIPTION OF THE BUILDING

The building, which faces on Garden Road just by the Peak Tramway Station, is an adaptation of the Renaissance style of architecture, the outside walls being in rough cast. It has a frontage on the Garden Road of about 105 feet, with three storeys on that side and four on the frontage facing the tramway. On this side there is a fairly large garden which has been considerably improved by the covering in of the nullah which runs by, this work being done by permission of the Government. Some difficulty was experienced in getting a good foundation in consequence of the slope down to the tramway being steep and owing to the nature of the soil. It was discovered that the earth had probably been placed there many years before and was not solid enough to permit of a good foundation. However, on digging deeply good hard ground was found.

The basement of the building, facing the tramway, is enclosed only on two sides, and being 65 feet by 30 feet, will be used as a recreation ground; also as a drill ground for the Girl Guides, who have their own lavatories, etc. The rooms on the ground floor are very commodious. The lecture and concert hall is 65 by 30 feet and is fitted with a raised platform, above which is hung a portrait of Lady May. The reading and writing room is very tastefully furnished. Afternoon teas will be served in the large room, and members are allowed to bring in their gentlemen friends. On this floor there are also the pantries, which are fitted with a hand lift communicating with the kitchens below. On the first floor are the day and committee rooms, and here again the design shows that utility was the chief aim. The day rooms are fitted with folding partitions and may easily be converted into a single large room. It is here that various societies will meet, each having their own room. The library is also on this floor and contains a good collection of books. Another feature is the fine verandah on the tramway side of the building, from which a grand view is obtainable. The upper floor is devoted to bedrooms, which have been simply, but effectively furnished. The bathrooms are also of a good design.

There can be no doubt that the Helena May Institute will supply a long-felt want in the Colony. The small annual subscription will make it within reach of all European girls and women who may meet there. It will take in a large measure, the place of the YWCA which institution at one time had a room in the Colony. The idea of establishing a YWCA hostel, apparently not meeting with universal approval, the idea of an Institute was mooted, the result being the present handsome building. When the scheme was made public, Mr Ellis Kadoorie, with his characteristic generosity and public spiritedness, came forward with an offer of $15,000, which would cover half the cost of the building, on the condition that the remainder would be collected within two years. With this encouraging commencement, the ladies concerned entered into their task with avidity, and in a few days they received the required amount from another generous citizen, in the person of Mr. Ho Kom Tong. Thus the money necessary was raised, and the site in Garden Road was secured building operations being quickly commenced to designs by Messrs. Denison, Ram and Gibbs. Mr. Ellis Kadoorie supplemented his munificent gift by undertaking to furnish the building throughout.

In her diary Iris May made a brief and factual entry "...went all over the building, which is ripping, specially the bedrooms."[50]

The Original Benefactors

Ellis Kadoorie, the major benefactor, came to Hong Kong in 1883. His brother Elly (father of Lawrence and grandfather of Michael) had travelled from Baghdad to Shanghai in 1880 to join the Iraqi-Jewish firm of David Sassoon & Co., which traded in India, China and Britain, and other brothers may have joined them. They were thrifty and industrious and this meant that they could in turn be generous. China Light & Power was founded in 1903 and succes-

sive generations of the Kadoorie family have been involved with it. By 1906 the brothers were able to buy a major shareholding in Hongkong Hotels, and by 1914 Ellis was on the company's board. He gave over $500,000 to charitable causes before the outbreak of the First World War, including scholarships for underprivileged Indian children. A school for Indians was named after him and was eventually taken over by the government. In 1917, in recognition of his charitable commitments and his support for an appeal to buy war planes from Britain, he was knighted.[51] He died in 1922.

Ho Kom Tong was born in 1866 and was a very colourful character who came from the best known Eurasian family of the time. His brother was the legendary Jardine's compradore Sir Robert Ho Tung. Another brother was Ho Fook – the grandfather of Macau magnate Stanley Ho. As "go-betweens" with Jardine's they were able to make their fortunes quickly, but were known also for their philanthropy. In 1894, during the bubonic plague, Ho Kom Tong made cash donations, distributed medicines and paid for coffins when necessary. In 1904 he established public dispensaries, and during the typhoon of 1906 raised funds and influenced the Government to build the Yaumatei typhoon shelter. He had been a school friend of Sun Yat Sen at Queen's College, and he aided victims of the Boxer rebellion. He also founded the local branch of the St John Ambulance Brigade and helped to build the Kwong Wah Hospital. In 1914 he built Kom Tong Hall on Lower Castle Road, Mid-levels a 2,500-sq m home that is one of the few surviving Western-style houses from its era. Its architecture was part of a wave of classical revival style emanating from England in the 19th century. Ho Kom Tong was decorated with a CBE for his charitable work. He died in 1950. The Hall became a Grade 2 listed building in 1990 and is in the process of being restored by the government to house the Sun Yat Sen Museum, due to open in 2007. His extended family produced a book in 2003, *Ho Kom Tong - A Man for All Seasons,* and presented a copy to the Helena May.

Sir Robert Ho Tung was born in 1862 and had a Chinese mother and European father. He made his fortune from land purchase and development, and supported the 1911 Chinese Revolution. Along with his wife, Lady Clara Lin-kok, he promoted Buddhism and education in Hong Kong. The Sir Robert Ho Tung Charitable Fund was set up in 1956 and continues to support various welfare projects in the community. The Mays attended the wedding of his

From left, Ellis Kadoorie, Henry May and Ho Kom Tong at the opening

daughter Victoria, and as Mrs Lo she joined the Council of the Helena May after the Japanese Occupation. Connections with the family have continued with great-grandchildren being current members.

Lau Chu Pak is described in the list of jurors for 1910 as "Assistant, A. S. Watson & Co., Queen's Road Central." He was also a Legislative Councillor, being first appointed as an unofficial member in March 1914. He was appointed as a member of the Authorised Architects committee in October 1914, and perhaps was able to help in some way with the actual building of the Helena May. He is also noted for having paid tribute to Henry May at a joint meeting of the Executive and Legislative Councils when Henry's retirement was announced in 1919.[52] He died in 1922.

Chan Kai Ming had been appointed to the Sanitary Board (forerunner of the Urban Council) in April 1912, and in October 1915 he was appointed a member of the Court of the University of Hong Kong along with Ellis Kadoorie. In 1918 he became a member of the Legislative Council but died the following year.

Ivor Gourgey is described in the list of jurors for 1910 as "Assistant, E. S. Kadoorie & Co., Castle Steps".

OTHER NEWS AROUND THE TIME OF THE OPENING

The edition of the 12 page *South China Morning Post* on 13 September 1916 had on its front page an article about 'a man who stopped a bullet', but as usual for the time most of the space was taken up with advertisements – for lamps, cement, wire, rope, disinfectant, insurance, loans, French lessons, a hotel, an optician, piano tuning, jewellery, a war souvenir brooch and post office notices. News of the opening of the Helena May Institute only came on page 6.

On other pages, the Wing On company advertised itself as 'the shop where you can buy anything from a needle to an anchor' (perhaps modelling itself on Harrods in London); a large shipment of 'choicest ham and American sweets' had just arrived at the Alexandra cafe; and a 'mistress' was fined $50 for ill-treating her young servant girl. Ladies' hats, flowers and ostrich feathers were to be auctioned, and various flats, offices and houses were available to let. A. S. Watson advertised a 'home remedy which works wonders making scrawny underdeveloped men and women plump' and Lane Crawford had their end of season sale. There are several advertisements for hotel rooms, and most of two pages are given over to news of ship arrivals and departures. For entertainment there was boxing, theatre, a full military band and 'amusement without discomfort' at the Palisade 'out-of-door-pictures' beside the Kowloon Post Office. And there was news of the war in Europe.

The population in this year was estimated to be 528,010, of whom only 13,400 were non-Chinese (2.5 per cent). The Governor, who was also Commander-in-Chief and Vice-Admiral, received £4,800 annual salary, two houses (Government House and Mountain Lodge) and an entertainment allowance of £1,200.[53]

Prostitutes had come to Hong Kong from America and Europe because of the gender imbalance due to the large presence of the army garrison, the Royal Navy and merchant ships. Of course none of these ladies would be allowed to stay at the Helena May Institute. During the War all European prostitutes were supposedly deported as a 'precaution'.[54]

Being thin was held responsible for unhappiness and the Post reported a health-journal editor telling a reader: 'If you only had a reserve of fat, this would give a quieting and reassuring influence to the vital forces. You would then be happy, contented and optimistic. The proper distribution of fat on the body and limbs makes all the difference between beauty and ugliness, and you envy your plump friends.'[55]

The *Report on the Botanical and Forestry Department for the Year 1916* gives details of the work that had been done at the Lower Albany Nursery and on the Peak Tramway Banks on completion of the Institute. Poinsettias and other flowering shrubs were planted as well as 15 young Eucalyptus trees.[56]

ENDNOTES

1 Simpson, 2005
2 Cooper, 2001, p.62
3 Strobel, 1991, p.25
4 Strobel, 1991, p.xi-xiii
5 Gartrell, 1984, p.169
6 Strobel, 1991, p.15
7 Stark, 1932, p.59
8 Hoe, 1991, p.133
9 Hoe, 1991, p.158
10 Trollope, 1983, p.127
11 Jarrett, 1933 to 1935, p.1101
12 Hoe, 1991, p.174
13 Hoe, 1991, p.172-4, p.203
14 Hoe, 1991, p.175
15 Hoe, 1991, p.172
16 Brownfoot, 1984, p.200
17 Barker, 1996
18 Barker, 1996, p.40
19 Barker, 1996, p.47
20 Hoe, 1991, p.140
21 Hoe, 1991, p.126-132
22 www.matilda.org/mat_background_past.asp (17 March 2005)
23 Strobel, 1991, p.41
24 Hoe, 1991, p.180
25 Speech by Henry May at the opening ceremony
26 Speech by Henry May at the opening ceremony
27 YWCA Report for 1912, p.5
28 YWCA Report for 1912, p.4
29 YWCA Report for 1912, p.5
30 YWCA Report for 1912, p.1
31 Veronica Johnston, personal communication to Esther Morris, 12 April 2006
32 YWCA Report for 1912 p.4
33 The Helena May booklet by Robyn Mclean and Rosemary Lee, 1994, p.3
34 *From Fallen Women to Helena May* - a talk given by Susanna Hoe 28 Feburary 1991 – notes p.5
35 http://ywca.org.hk/eng/abouty_2.aspx
36 Severn – referred to in Hoe, 1991, p.181
37 The Helena May booklet by Robyn Mclean and Rosemary Lee, p.4
38 Historical and Statistical Abstract of the Colony of Hong Kong, 1841-1930
39 A Short History of the Helena May Institute, 1934 reprinted in 1979, p.12
40 A Short History of the Helena May Institute, 1934 reprinted in 1979, p.13
41 The Helena May booklet by Robyn Mclean and Rosemary Lee, 1994, p.4
42 A Short History of the Helena May Institute, 1934 reprinted in 1979, p.13-14
43 The Helena May booklet by Robyn Mclean and Rosemary Lee, 1994, p.6-7
44 A Short History of the Helena May Institute, 1934 reprinted in 1979, p.14.
45 Report of the Director of Public Works for the Year 1914, p.18 - http://sunzi1.lib.hku.hk/hkgro/view/a1914/235.pdf
46 Speech by Henry May at the opening ceremony
47 http://centenary.scmp.com/cenarts
48 Hoe, 1991, p.190
49 http://centenary.scmp.com/cenarts/mp1913/zzzi1ijmwkd.html
50 Diary excerpts courtesy of Veronica Johnston, youngest daughter of Iris
51 Fionnuala McHugh in the Post Magazine 30 Nov 2003
52 Sayer, 1975, p.122-123
53 The Blue Book 1916
54 Hosford, 2002, p.112
55 http://centenary.scmp.com/cenarts/mp1913/zzzi1ijmwkd.html
56 http://sunzi1.lib.hku.hk/hkgro/view/a1916/294.pdf

F G H I J
K L M N O
P Q R S T
W X YZ

LETTERS

3. The First 30 Years: 1916 to 1945

Although records about the Helena May Institute from this period were largely lost or destroyed during the Japanese Occupation of Hong Kong, we have been able to piece together information from documents that had been taken to Britain, from newspaper and government reports, and from other resources that relate to the people who were involved with the place during these years. These latter in particular add some flavour of the times. For the rest we must use our imaginations.

Besides the description provided at the opening ceremony, we know that in 1916 a resident Matron was engaged and that afternoon teas would be served in the large room, and gentleman friends could be invited! The first Company of Girl Guides had been founded that year at the Victoria British School and thus they share the anniversary year with the Helena May. A front page newspaper report[1] highlights the number of women replacing men in the labour market, and the Government's *Administrative Report* is very informative about the charitable work being done by women. It notes that the Eyre Diocesan Refuge is one of those institutions 'recognised and encouraged, but not to any considerable extent supported by Government.'[2] Further:

The Queen Mary's Needlework Guild, the Hong Kong Association of War Workers, and other bodies of ladies engaged in war work were unremitting in their labours throughout the year with the result that many thousands of articles of clothing, bandages, etc., were dispatched to the various war centres for the use of the troops and hospitals.[3]

The Peak Tram, covered nullah and rear of the Helena May 1918

The Hong Kong University had its first Congregation on 14 December. An entry in the diary[4] kept by Iris May records the event:

...All family to University for Conferring of Degrees Ceremony. Crowds there, men in their robes (if they had any) & women in their best clothes. I wore my new coat, skirt & hat. Tea'd at little tables & then all assembled in big hall. Procession of people in robes, who sat on the stage. Dad's robes (he's Chancellor) are gorgeous. Anthem - full military band and large choir, Phoebe among them - sung from gallery.

Friday 15 December: Last night after University Phoebe & I dined with Georgette & went on to H[elena] M[ay] I[nstitute] where we played games with some of the shop girls. Mrs Gibson there too. Phoebe sang & Georgette played for her...

Helena was President of both the Queen Mary's Needlework Guild and the Hong Kong Association of Women War Workers, and they were the subject of 'special mention' by Henry, as Governor, in the Legislative Council on 29 March 1917. A number of groups were involved including: The City Hall Work Party; Our Little Bit Society, Kowloon; the Wesleyan Church Work party; and the Mothers' Union Work party. The report notes that bandage making classes were held at the Helena May Institute under Mrs Jordan, and also at the Peak Club, the United Services Recreation Club and the Catholic Women's League. Various other groups and their efforts to raise funds were also praised in a stirring speech that ended by quoting Lloyd George's appeal to the nation to support the (British) Government.

FIRST WORLD WAR ENDS

1918 was an eventful year with the Great War ending and, in Britain, women over the age of 30 being given the vote. In Hong Kong at Chinese New Year at Happy Valley racecourse, where the May family were in attendance as Iris was due to present the Ladies' Plate,[5] a fire killed 600 people. By the end of the year the worldwide influenza epidemic had killed about 20 million people.

As noted in Chapter One, in September Henry took the family on leave to Canada. He tendered his resignation as Governor by telegram on 15 January 1919.[6] He and Helena would never see Hong Kong again. An album of Hong Kong Views was assembled for Helena by some of her friends and an announcement was made that it was on view at the Helena May Institute until 20 September.[7] The inscription read:

A small souvenir of Hongkong for Lady May – with the good wishes and affection of a few of her friends who are still in the Colony. Hong Kong, August 1919

The album had blackwood covers adorned with silver inlay and leather binding 'making a book that should keep its condition for many years'. Inside there was a watercolour painting of the harbour at twilight by a Mrs Macpherson, and 50 sepia toned photographs including 'the best the Colony has to offer in scenery, as well as characteristic Hongkong views'. Their collection 'had afforded a labour of love to the committee of ladies, headed by Mrs Stabb.' There were also over three pages of names.

A further newspaper announcement a week later[8] stated that it was possible for more names to be added. These were to be sent to the Hon. Secretary at the Helena May Institute or to Mrs Stabb at 117 The Peak. 'The subscription is any sum up to $1.' The Institute's new office bearers were also announced: President, Lady Rees Davies; Vice-President, Mrs J. H. Kemp; Hon. Treasurer, Mrs H. E. Pollock; and Hon. Secretary, Mrs A. Mackenzie. After running for three years the situation was 'satisfactory':

Boarders and travellers have patronised the Institute in increasing numbers, and frequently the accommodation has been taxed to its utmost limit. The membership has suffered somewhat owing to so many ladies being away on holiday and some have left the Colony for good. Their places, however, are being gradually taken by new members. The Institute is one of the leading centres of women's work in the Colony, and one of the few social institutions open to and entirely run by ladies. The subscription is a moderate one and includes the use of an excellent library and reading room to which additions are continually being made by regular supplies from Home.

During the year, three of the classrooms on the first floor were converted into bedrooms.[9] The likelihood is that these were shared rooms, and so a number of young women would have benefited. This was also the year that marked another milestone for women in Britain, when they were able to gain entry to the Civil Service. An important event for travellers of the future was the first transatlantic flight from Canada to Ireland.

In 1920 the Chinese YWCA was founded, the Repulse Bay Hotel opened, the American Club was founded and George Bernard Shaw visited Hong Kong, and Mr Ho Yum Chuen joined the Helena May staff. His job was to go to market to buy food. Within four years he had been promoted to chief waiter, and he held this position until the Japanese Occupation in 1941, when he left for Canton.

Another interesting figure enters the Helena May story at this time. Novelist Stella Benson, aged 28, made her first visit to Hong Kong in February 1920, as part of her extensive travels from Britain that had started in June 1918.[10] She had friends and family connections and so, despite a lack of qualifications for the job, she gained a position as a teacher to a class of 50 Chinese and Eurasian boys aged 10 to 23 in a Church mission school. She taught them 'all branches of human knowledge (except mathematics) for a hundred and fifty Hongkong dollars a month.' The boys apparently loved her unusual style and remembered her long afterwards. She was also part of the British social scene, going to parties and dances, though she tired of that society and the pleurisy she suffered from returned. As a result she left for Peking in May of the same year.[11] There she met her husband-to-be, Shaemas (James) O'Gorman Anderson, who worked for Chinese Maritime Customs. It was with him that she returned to Hong Kong in 1930 and made her impact on the Helena May.

Members of the Helena May Institute were reminded in newspaper announcements on 25 January 1921 of the Devotional Meeting to be conducted by the Bishop of Victoria at half-past ten that morning, and that Mr Crock's lecture on *Early Man* had been postponed, whereas the lecture on *Elements of Gardening* had been cancelled altogether.

This was a decennial census year[12] and the count was made on 24 April. The City of Victoria – 'a term hardly known to ordinary residents, and rarely heard or seen except in maps and official reports'– now had a population of 323,273. Presumably the residents of the Helena May Institute would have been included in this figure.

The Local Population in 1921

The total non-Chinese population was 12,856, with those of pure-European descent estimated to be around 5,000. Reference is made, in this section, to the 'unusually large number of young married women at present resident in the colony' and the consequent high birth rate. We do not know the nationalities or occupations of the residents at the Institute, but the ladies who were just social members, and not residents, were quite likely to be mostly, if not exclusively, British. Overall European men greatly outnumbered women between the two world wars. This was partly due to the fact that most major companies and the services stipulated that men were not allowed to marry until their late twenties at least. Government servants were not allowed to be married during their first four-year tour and Hong Kong and Shanghai Banking Corporation expatriates were not allowed to marry for the first ten years.[13]

In this census the non-Chinese population is divided into four categories and in total there were 889 females listed as having occupations: British (304), Japanese (279), Portuguese (161) and others (145). It would be interesting to know which of these women resided at the Helena May. Amongst the working British females, there were 80 typists and stenographers, 46 working in education, 43 governesses and nurses in personal service, 27 in the nursing profession, 18 telephonists, 12 clerks, 11 listed under religion and 10 under tailoring. Other occupations had fewer than 10 women each.

This was a time when there were a number of Japanese merchants in the colony and it is noticeable from the table shown that under 'entertainment' is the occupation 'prostitute' and all 139 were Japanese. Another 88 Japanese females are listed as being in 'personal service' (at both homes and other establishments), 21 were in the professions (including 5 in massage) and 13 were employed in the manufacturing of clothing. It is unlikely that any of these ladies were associated with the Helena May.

Amongst the Portuguese females, 50 were typists and stenographers, 38 operated telephones, and another 22 were in commerce related activities. 18 were employed in personal service and 15 are listed under religion. Of the other non-Chinese females, half of them (73) were involved in religion, a total of 22 were in personal service and nursing, 15 in education, and six were employed manufacturing cigars!

This was also a landmark year as the first female student was admitted to the University of Hong Kong - Rachel Irving, daughter of the Director of Education and official Legislative Council Member, Mr E.A. Irving. Later Irene Ho Tung, daughter of Sir Robert Ho Tung, also entered. In contrast, London University had been granting degrees to women since 1878.

At the Helena May Institute there were ongoing improvements and Sir Ellis Kadoorie gave $25,000 towards the cost.[14] Sadly he passed away on 24 February 1922 – just 18 days after Henry May – and so ended a long era of association with Hong Kong for both of them. In May of the same year Mr Lau Chu Pak, another Helena May benefactor, also died. At the Institute a resident Secretary was added to the staff, and the extension work was completed and opened to view on 21 June. A newspaper report[15] indicates that:

The most striking feature of the innovations is the conversion into a spacious dining hall of a large and formerly open basement. The dining hall has been fitted up specially with electric power for cinematographic purposes and it is proposed to use the hall for lectures and other forms of entertainment.

Part of the basement has been turned into a splendid up-to-date kitchen replacing one which was far from adequate to the needs of the institution. Above the kitchen are Chinese quarters, comfortable, light and airy.

A new library, larger and better than the old one, has been constructed and now houses some 6,000 volumes. The old library with the former Committee room has been transformed into three bedrooms; whilst the former dining room which was anything but large enough for that purpose now makes a convenient sitting room.

The building is fitted up with a modern external safety staircase to which has been added an extra balcony. Altogether by reason of these alterations and the extension of the building the Helena May Institute has been very considerably improved.

Members of the Helena May Institute and the public generally are promised a full programme for the winter, giving the gratifying assurance that full use is to be made of the Institute in the colony's social life. All manner of fixtures are projected. From late October there will be musicales and tea dances, and teas for mercantile marine officers. A special feature will be a popular lecture by Rev. E. Dewstoe of Canton on "Street Processions", while two lectures on astronomical subjects by Rev. J. Kink Maconochie are also promised. There will also be children's hours, with talks on butterflies and such attractive subjects, cinematographic displays, etc.

For the more seriously minded there will be the reading circles gatherings in the mornings, cookery instruction, religious work, and lectures. Some open lectures on science, history and literature have been promised by Prof. Barney, Prof. Romanis Lee and Prof. Simpson of Hongkong University.

The provision for children will interest a great number. This department is being conducted by Mr Temple Bevan. It is proposed during coming winter months to hold a weekly singing class with a view to stimulating and fostering in children's minds a sense of appreciation of good music. The programme will be varied as much as possible and will include pianoforte recitals, lectures on composers and appreciation of music. The classes are to be regarded as more in the nature of an instructive entertainment than a lesson in singing.

The Institute was in the news again when a different sort of recreation was reported on 19 August. Four Chinese men had been caught bathing in the nullah outside. There had been frequent complaints about this sort of behaviour "which invariably occurred opposite the Institute" and as the men were "improperly clad" they were fined $4 or could spend five days in jail. The Magistrate was told that it would not have mattered so much "if the defendants had kept themselves under the bridge, where they were concealed from view. Instead they chased each other about."[16]

The tennis court was laid in 1923, and hopefully there were no more distractions for the ladies when they were playing! However they were heading for exciting times in other ways as the first aeroplane landed on a grass strip at Kai Tak airport in 1924. In October of that year 19-year-old Marjorie Angus arrived in Kowloon. She came out in the more usual way - on a P & O ship - to visit her father, who was a Captain with the Douglas Steamship Company. The return fare was £120 and the sea journey took six weeks each way. She stayed with her family at the Empress Lodge on Mody Road in Tsimshatsui. At the time the big 'hongs' rented houses for their bachelor staff to share and Marjorie found that being a young single woman she was in much demand:

...in the 1920s... I think that we lived very well. Of course it may have helped that at that time we had about ten men to one girl. What parties they used to give! ...When the P & O ship came out from home bringing girls to be married, the wedding had to take place within 36 hours of the ship's arrival. (Unless the girl had a family to go to or friends to stay with.)

This was the time when many single girls came to Hong Kong as part of the so-called 'fishing fleet' – in search of eligible bachelors. Marjorie worked as an assistant in a curio shop called the Jade Tree, and tells us that she could not remember ever seeing a Chinese girl in a foreign office before 1930. Her book includes a photograph of a tennis party at the Helena May in that year.[17]

Social Unrest

Considerable social and political unrest occurred in China during the 1920s and this inevitably affected Hong Kong. In 1925, the year of Dr Sun Yat-sen's death, Hong Kong experienced a general strike-instigated, according to Colonial and Foreign Office officials by 'Bolshevist agitators' from across the border. Domestic servants and club employees walked off the job and many crossed the border into China. It was estimated that between 19 June and the middle of July 250,000 people left Hong Kong. It seems very likely that the Institute lost some members of staff at this time and it was not until late October that daily life returned to normal, when many of those who had fled started drifting back.

In November Cecil Clementi, an old friend of the May family, returned to Hong Kong as the 17th Governor, with his wife Penelope. Before the war her father, Cresswell John Eyres, had been the Naval Commodore, and she was very much an outdoor type. Part of her legacy is Lady Clementi's Ride – a walk above Wanchai Gap, and as we shall see later she has also entered the folklore of the Helena May.

The Society for Overseas Settlement of Women Annual Report of 1926 states that in that year a large number of British women emigrated to Canada (18,080), Australia (15,607), New Zealand (5,929), India (3,179) and other parts of the British Empire (2,286). Presumably some found their way to Hong Kong. The Peninsula Hotel, owned by the Hong Kong and Shanghai Hotels group, in which both Robert Ho Tung and the Kadoorie family had interests, opened in 1928. At the Helena May Institute a part-time Librarian was appointed. The following year saw further changes:

... the addition of a new office, with verandah, for the Secretary, the old office being converted into a members' cloakroom. The removal of the former Cloakroom gave extra space for the pantry. A fire escape was also constructed to ensure the safety of residents on the upper floor.[18]

The Kowloon Branch of the Helena May Institute

On 29 November 1929 Lady Clementi presided over the Annual Meeting of the Institute, which was attended by 20 subscriber members. She announced that the Council had taken the 'progressive step of renting premises in Kowloon in order to further the activities of the Institute in the rapidly developing mainland'. This was a far-sighted move on the part of the Council and one which

THE HELENA MAY.

Branch to Be Formed in Kowloon.

"A BIG DAUGHTER."

That the Council of the Helena May had taken the progressive step of renting premises in Kowloon in order to further the activities of the Institute in the rapidly developing mainland, was the welcome news given by Lady Clementi to subscribers at the annual meeting of the Institute held yesterday, when she presided over an attendance of twenty members.

Lady Clementi said that there had been a good deal of discussion in the Council since the publication of the annual report as to the extension of the work of the Institute in Kowloon, which was now grow-

recognised the impact projects such as the Kowloon Tong Garden Suburb were to have on the size of the population across the harbour. A 'rather charming house' with six rooms had been rented for one year at No. 8 Aimai Villas, facing the Kowloon Cricket Club in Austin Road. It was the intention that it would be made into a hostel 'as much like the Institute as possible', and Lady Clementi hoped 'that it would encourage many women in Kowloon to join the Helena May' which 'represented the women of Hong Kong, and they wanted it to represent them all.'

The Honorary Secretary, Mrs Strachey, presented the report and the balance sheet, which stated there were 455 members with 77 new members joining during the year. A further 10 quarterly members were not included in this total. 'A Bronze Tablet had been placed in the hall of the Club to commemorate the original donors and the purpose for which the Club stands.' It bore the following inscription:

The Helena May Institute for Women was opened on the 12th of September 1916. It was founded mainly through the generosity of Sir Ellis Kadoorie, Kt., and Mr Ho Kom-tong, OBE, assisted by many other subscribers, to commemorate the valuable service rendered to the colony by Helena, wife of Sir Henry May, GCMG, Governor of Hong Kong. This Institute stands as a means of furthering the Social Service to which Lady May devoted so much time and enthusiasm.

Unfortunately, according to his grandson, Anthony Mak[19], Ho Kom-tong was decorated with a CBE and not OBE as stated. The report continues:

By special request of the Religious Committee, a quiet room, with 8 ft. verandah, was built at the north east corner of the dining room. The Secretary's office is directly above this, the old office has been converted into a more convenient cloakroom with the most modern form of flush system. The old cloakroom was thrown into the pantry.

The exterior of the building was repainted. A fire escape, with patent extension, has been fixed at a cost of $860.00, and red lights for guidance to exits have been put in both corridors and on stairways. A raised platform has been put in the dining room for use at lectures. The lounge platform has been improved by the erection of a framework from which is hung a curtain, for use during concerts. A new Grotrian Steinway piano was bought and has proved a great asset. The old upright piano in the dining room was exchanged for a new one. Knives have been replaced, 6 doz. from Mappin and Webb, china and glass have been ordered and should arrive shortly. 50 new cane chairs were purchased.

There have been 17 resident boarders throughout the year and several travellers passing through. Eight to fifteen non-residents come for tiffins each day. During the year, 1 September 1928 to 31st August 1929, 420 new books have been added to the Library; of these, 12 were French novels. 70 juvenile books have been presented to the library. The music scores belonging to the Social Committee are not kept in the Library.'

Big Daughter newspaper clipping

An announcement appeared in a newspaper on 2 January 1930 for a concert that included the accomplished amateur pianist Mr Bowes-Smith, who had come to Hong Kong in 1920 via Shanghai to work for David Sassoon & Co. Ltd. and founded the Hong Kong Musical Society in 1929. His wife, Marjory, was a singer who also appeared in various operatic productions including Iolanthe and Madam Butterfly.

A WRITER'S VIEW OF HONG KONG

Stella Benson – now Mrs Anderson – accompanied her husband on a 12-day voyage from Nanning in May 1930 and arrived back in Hong Kong: '...a good place for men, a good place for a certain kind of woman, but a place Stella regarded with fear and contempt.'[20] In the event society was 'less tiresome than she had feared' and she 'rather enjoyed the large receptions'. The official residence of the Deputy Commissioner of Customs was a pleasant villa on the Peak and good food was in plentiful supply. Sometimes they were given the use of the Commissioner's yacht and being out on the water was something the couple both enjoyed. Nevertheless she found relationships superficial and complained in her letter of 31 January 1931 to Lady Eileen Orde[21] '...we can't find any body who isn't Refined – or rather, the few people who are just going or just gone.' On 29 March she wrote: 'The general REFANEMENT and CULTCHA would amuse you... as a spectacle (it is a little exhausting from any other point of view).' Her preference was for the company of men 'because she would rather listen to risqué stories than chit-chat about servants, schools, and the price of comestibles.'[22]

As Librarian at the Helena May Institute, Stella was able to shrewdly observe some of the behaviour of the European community. In an article entitled 'On Using a Library' in the *St. John's Review*[23] she tells of members who would often send a coolie with a note 'Please give bearer two books'. In response she 'became quite callous about this method of trial by coolie, since it is Hong Kong's most usual method of selecting reading matter' and notes 'but I always hope that the books I send will disappoint the subscribers who receive them, and so eventually spur them into greater fastidiousness.'

She was at the height of her own powers as a writer and put a lot of effort into launching subversive attacks on the government for licensing prostitutes: 'Which is a ridiculous thing to do in a place like this. But this is an out-of-the way silly Govt, though a rather nice tired old Governor (Sir William Peel) wrote her husband in a letter to Eileen in June.[24] Stella, as a former suffragette, was spearheading the movement and working hard, along with a Mrs Forster and some government officials, 'attacking the licensing of harlots, usually children and slaves, for the use of British soldiers and sailors.'[25] She made a report to the League of Nations Society in Hong Kong.

Meanwhile the Kowloon branch of the Helena May Institute was duly opened by Lady Clementi, for which Mr Ho Kom Tong and Mr Tang Shiu Kin (another well-known benefactor in Hong Kong) donated $1,000 and $500 respectively for its upkeep.

1931 was another decennial census year and in Hong Kong this was taken on 7 March.[26] The introduction to the final report notes the difference between the enumerations in different years and that the 1921 census was 'not so complete' as in 1911, with several questions missing so that the non-Chinese population was only classified by nationality and not by race. This new census found that for all non-Chinese persons there were 765.54 females per 1,000 males, but there were variations within different groups – fewer Indian women, and more Eurasian and local Portuguese. Including the defence forces and mercantile marine caused the proportion to fall to 385.55 women per 1,000 men.

The table of occupations has three categories of nationalities – (i) Europeans & USA citizens, (ii) other non-Chinese, (iii) Chinese – each of which is divided into male and female. Most non-Chinese females are in the category 'retired or not gainfully employed' – leaving only (i) 716 out of 3,721 and (ii) 550 out of 4,160 in paid employment. If we look just at category (i), by far the largest number were in 'professional occupations' (372). This comprised nurses, teachers and members of religious bodies. Next were 'clerks, draughtsmen & typists' (195), 'personal service' (76) and 'commercial, finance and insurance occupations' (35). There were also 14 women engaged in 'entertainments and sports'.

The Lives of Single Girls

Most of the single girls would live with their parents, and we can only speculate as to which of these women stayed at the Helena May Institute or so-called 'virgins' retreat', where, according to Marjorie Angus, a strict maternal code was enforced and Lady Clementi, '...a notorious prude', read all the books bought for the Helena May library. 'On finding any reference to a kiss or a cuddle ... the book was removed.'[27] One such book was Blue Lagoon (later made into a film), the withdrawal of which from the library shelves made it an instant best-seller!

Although motoring was approaching its heyday in Britain and the first Highway Code had been published the previous year, there were still more rickshaws and sedan chairs being used in Hong Kong than cars in 1932.[28] The legalised brothels with regular health inspections were being closed down because the government had a change of heart. The *Hong Kong Telegraph* reported in an editorial that 'Hong Kong's greatest peril today lies in the fact that there is a chronic shortage of the female sex.' Prostitutes had moved in precisely because of the gender imbalance due to the presence of the army garrison, Royal Navy and merchant ships.[29] They were now being driven underground and as a result venereal disease became rife amongst the troops.

Marjorie Angus holds Lady Clementi responsible (for the closures), while others maintained that the closure was the result of pressure from the League of Nations and Britain's first woman member of parliament, Lady Astor. Eric Himsworth on the other hand is convinced that the clamp-down was due to the efforts of a triumvirate of powerful wives: Mrs. Wolfe married to the Inspector-General of Police, Mrs Tratman, married to the Secretary for Chinese Affairs, and Lady Southorn, wife of the Colonial Secretary.[30]

The *South China Morning Post* of 4 July 1933 ran its regular 'Old Hong Kong' column by 'Colonial', which recalled the day 21 years earlier when an assassination attempt was made on Henry May, whom the writer describes as 'one of the most interesting personalities the Colony has ever had in an administrative post.' It is also noted that the Helena May Institute commemorates his wife.

On the same page of the newspaper is an article entitled 'Wives' Rights' about the government in the US recognising the right of wives to the bulk of a man's wages. Federal conservation workers were having five-sixths of the money they earned mailed directly to their wives. Meanwhile, in Hong Kong, the Peninsula Hotel was about to start dinner dances and musical dinners in the Roof Garden for the summer season; and you could buy 'Bata' shoes in Gloucester Building: $3.90 for a pair of ladies' leather slippers.

Agnes C. Wolfe was President, and Evelyn Grist was Honorary Secretary to the Council of the Helena May Institute in 1934. The short history that they signed for that year gives the following information:

The Hostel affords accommodation and a comfortable home for business women at a reasonable cost, the scale of charges being made on a sliding basis, according to the salary and income of the applicant. A special rate is granted to Missionaries, many of whom visit the Colony for a holiday during the summer months, and limited numbers of rooms are kept available for travellers. Stewardesses on ships are also made especially welcome.

Concerts or entertainments are held fortnightly during the winter, and the dining room is frequently the scene of most interesting lectures. The Christian Fellowship Meetings, to which members of the public are most warmly welcomed, are held every Friday morning at 10.30 o'clock, and the Institute rooms are also thrown open to the committees of various charities in the colony. Special facilities offered to members are: (I) the hiring of the matshed at Repulse Bay, and (II) the tennis court in the garden: the library is an important factor in the amenities of the Institute.

The entire management is in the hands of the sixteen Shareholders who comprise the Council.

The Report of the Director of Public Works for the year lists various completed projects under the section entitled 'Communications'. This included

THE LIBRARIAN IS DELAYED
VE APOLOGISE FOR ANY INCONVENIENCE

widening of the approach path to 'Tanderagee' (a house on the hill) and a section of Garden Road (from about the Helena May Institute to Macdonnell Road) and laying a new type of non-skid slab footpath.

Nylon was invented in 1935. The significance of this for women cannot be underestimated – much excitement was generated by nylon stockings! As noted earlier, concerts were held regularly at the Institute, and during the early part of the year many of these were again given by Mr Aubrey M. and Mrs K. Marjory Bowes-Smith. The programme for the piano and vocal recital on 24 January cost 10 cents and included Frederick Mason on the piano. The fulsome press report notes that:

The Finale was vigorous and inspiring and the audience was not slow to acclaim it. It was a pity, but it is excusable, that there should have been applause from part of the audience between the movements of the Sonata. It spoils the connectedness of the work.[31]

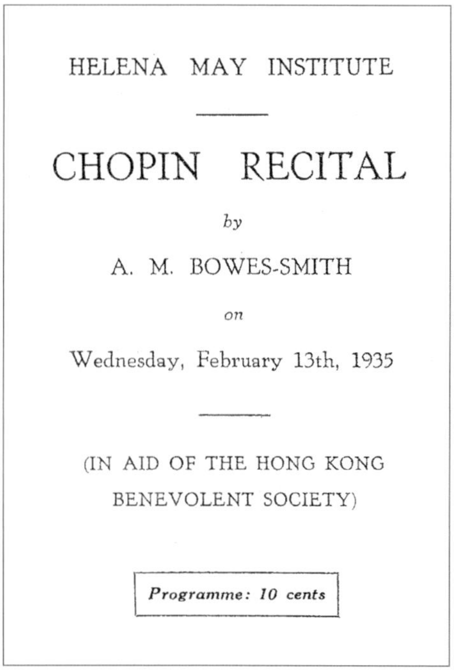
HELENA MAY INSTITUTE

CHOPIN RECITAL

by

A. M. BOWES-SMITH

on

Wednesday, February 13th, 1935

(IN AID OF THE HONG KONG BENEVOLENT SOCIETY)

Programme: 10 cents

On 13 February the talented Mr Bowes-Smith gave a solo Chopin recital. Again the press reports praised the performance of this businessman with musical and literary talents. Among those present were Sir Thomas and Lady Southorn, and the proceeds of the evening were going to the Hong Kong Benevolent Society '...a charity which makes a wide appeal'. Sadly Mr Bowes-Smith died in September of the same year after a short illness, aged just 42. Other people then appeared on the concert programmes – notably Dr L. T. Ride of the University of Hong Kong.

1937 was another bad year for Hong Kong as on 2 September a severe typhoon caused huge waves that killed 5,000 people on land (mainly in Shatin and Tai Po) and 10,000 on water. However, besides repairing damaged buildings, a number of Public Works projects were completed, including Queen Mary Hospital in Pokfulam, Wanchai Market, Stanley Market, and a shelter and car park at Garden Road. The widening of the portion of Garden Road between the Lower Peak Tram Station and the Helena May Institute was also completed.[32]

The Ministering League and Ministering Children's League had continued their work in Hong Kong and had a number of branches, including some in girls' schools. Their 1938 Annual Report notes the difficulties the Sino-Japanese conflict was causing, and records thanks to the Committee of the Helena May Institute for the use of rooms for the preparation and distribution of tins and baskets during the Flag Day on 18 February.

A report[33] on the Museum situation in various colonies notes:

Hong Kong represents the low-water mark in museum provision throughout the whole of the Empire, excepting the smaller islands of the Pacific and some of the more backward African territories... In the City Hall building there was a library consisting mainly of 19th century books in a very poor state; some of the more valuable books and many of the less valuable have been attacked by pests of all kinds, even the recent attempt of the British Museum authorities to have proper precautionary methods taken may prove to be too late. The University, the Hong Kong Club and the Helena May Institute have libraries open to their members... but apart from these there is little public library provision.

HELENA MAY

13th November, 1936

Programme

Doris Blair *(Soprano)* **Helen Lockhart** *(Contralto)*
Nura Kanis *(Pianoforte)* **Dr. L. T. Ride** *(Baritone)*
Accompanists:— **Genevieve Evelie - E. O'Neil Shaw.**

THE SECOND WORLD WAR BEGINS IN EUROPE

The Second World War started in Europe in September 1939 and Hong Kong became conscious of impending trouble from the Japanese. A great deal of publicity was given to air raid precautions, and construction of tunnels and shelters for the masses was planned. In July 1940 the Government ordered the registration of women and children in preparation for evacuation to Australia. On arrival there only those of pure European descent were accepted and Eurasians were returned to Hong Kong. A report in the *South China Morning Post* on 25 October is headlined: 'Women Want to Stay – Wife of Government Official Appeals to the Tribunal – Fails to Get Exemption. Mrs Kennedy-Skipton was making an 'impassioned plea' against the racial discrimination and said:

Being forced at a time of crisis to leave responsibility and duties behind was not a British attitude. There are women in the Colony of all nationalities some paid, some unpaid, who are giving freely of their time to essential social service. Hong Kong can ill afford to lose their work or the presence of even a few of them. It is they who are creating better understanding between races and nations.

However, life did still seem to be going on as normal at the Helena May Institute, as there are notices in the newspaper on 4 and 12 November about the Reel Club practice at 6pm on Wednesdays. On the latter date there is also a notice about the Helena May Religious Fellowship meeting on the 14th at 11am – Rev. J. E. Sandbach on 'Thinking Through to a New World.'

26 January 1941 was the centenary of the occupation of Hong Kong by the British. Sir Mark Young became Governor in September, and by now approximately 20 percent of the undergraduates at Hong Kong University were women. Notices in the Government Gazette of 3 October show the important contributions some expatriate women were making to the war effort.

The *South China Morning Post* of 28 November has a World of Women section with the headline: 'Higher Charges Necessary to Cover Working Losses of Helena May Institute'. Mrs G. D. R. Black, the Chairman, had announced at the Annual General Meeting that, as from the beginning of the new year, residents would have to pay a higher rate and other members were to have their subscriptions raised by 50 cents per month to help with running expenses. This was due to the decrease in income owing to many women being evacuated, and the increased cost of fuel. Fortunately the Institute had some investment income to draw on for maintenance, so the dining room and other public rooms, as well as the outside of the building, were being redecorated, and the covers of the lounge chairs were being replaced.

Other ladies present at the meeting were the Patroness, Lady MacGregor, Mesdames Dunlop, Hawkins, McLeod, Perdue, Pope, Pritchard, Puckle, Reynaud and White, Miss Gubbay (aunt of Muriel Gubbay, who was later to become Lady Kadoorie) and Miss J. Findlay, the Secretary. Her 'fine work' and 'willing cooperation', along with that of Mrs Groundwater, the Housekeeper, was recorded. There is also praise for the ladies who ran the library and 'do the work of a paid librarian' and regrets about those who have had to leave Hong Kong. Due to the situation there were no entertainments being run, 'but the Nursing Detachment of Hong Kong Volunteers organise monthly whist drives for the troops'. The Religious Committee was having difficulty holding its meetings due to 'the dearth of Clergy in the Colony'. The AGM ended with an auction of magazines, and it was hoped that some 'generous person' would purchase them for the troops, who had a 'crying need of literature'.

Those who read this page in the newspaper also would have seen a photograph of film star Anna Neagle at the microphone in an underground theatre in London used by the BBC and a report on the record number of Chinese couples who had married at the Registry. There are advertisements for a lipstick 'for lips with individual allure', Wright's Coal Tar soap and Pepsodent toothpaste and powder. Quail could be bought for 49 cents each and gammon ham was $1.20 per pound.

The Fall of Hong Kong

Within the next few weeks life became very different. On 7 December Japan attacked the US fleet in Pearl Harbour, Honolulu, and British planes on the ground were destroyed by the bombing of Kai Tak airport. The Japanese crossed the border into Hong Kong on the 8th. Some of the Hong Kong Volunteers, like Marjorie Bottomley's father,[34] had been mobilised in November, and more were called up now, amongst them Billy Gittens. His wife Jean, daughter of Sir Robert and Lady Clara Ho Tung, said goodbye and only ever saw him once again briefly.[35] 'The battle for Hong Kong had started'.[36] Japanese battalions crossed the harbour on the 18th. The Public Works Department took over the Helena May building.

A witness to the events was Andy Leiper, who was working for the Chartered Bank, and who, along with his wife Helen, was interned in Stanley Camp. He records[37] that on 22 December the Japanese were shelling Garden Road, and on the 23rd:

There was a dreadful shambles all around the Helena May Institute, where a stick of bombs had fallen. Collapsed walls and other debris blocked the path between the institute and the Peak Tram track and, as I clambered over this, I saw three dead bodies and various parts of others lying around.

Hong Kong was forced to surrender on Christmas Day. It is hard for those of us who have not experienced war to imagine the sorts of danger women were in at that time. At the St Stephen's College massacre in Stanley seven British nurses had been murdered. Others had been raped before being killed.[38] By 27 December the Japanese were reported to be molesting women and looting homes. The Japanese Director of Medical Sciences wanted a licensed quarter for prostitutes organized immediately. 'He said there were 40,000 troops on the island and they were a victorious army, and if some system were not started immediately there would be trouble for all of us. He would not be responsible for the safety of any woman, no matter what her nationality might be.'[39]

Between December 1941 and August 1945 an official English language newspaper called *The HongKong News* was published by Toshiko Eto and covered events in Hong Kong, China, East Asia and other countries. On 19 January 1942, it reports that 'the Japanese authorities have done a great deal to alleviate the distress of the population' and announces the reopening of banks to 'neutrals and Chinese'. In the same month there are reports of roads that had been bombed being repaired, tram services restarting, many shops resuming business, and hawkers doing a 'brisk trade' in fly-swatters due to the prevalence of this menace. There are also comments about 'disorganisation in the former British administration.'

Lieutenant General Isogai Rensuke was appointed governor of the 'Captured Territory' of Hong Kong in February and some of the 'established local Chinese elite (were) recruited, cajoled or forced', to serve in the administration.[40] In April the newspaper issues a reminder of the 11pm curfew and tells of the generosity of the authorities in allowing people access to their safe deposit boxes. From the 20th of the month Japanese names were adopted for various roads, though Garden Road does not appear on the published list.[41]

The new Government informed readers on 4 May that 'signs of a rapid return to prosperity' were to be seen in the 'flourishing' village of Taipo Market, and that the New Territories area was now very peaceful with Nipponese soldiers protecting people. A week later it was reported that night-life was being 'gradually restored to its former brilliance' with theatres giving Chinese stage shows and restaurants staying open later. On 15 May there is a report of a census that had been conducted by the District Bureau and the comment that many Chinese had returned to China. By the end of the year some 3,000 people who were not classified as Chinese were internees at Stanley Camp.

The Japanese army occupied Government House, St John's Cathedral, the Peninsula Hotel and many other well-known buildings. The Helena May was used to house troops and stable horses. Their Prime Minister issued a directive 'to find and export all valuable material kept by the British in this wealthy colony for use in Japan.'[42] Thus, in common with other places, most of the contents of the Helena May were looted. The portrait of Lady May disappeared during this time, but was replaced in 1950 by a photograph given by her daughters. The *HongKong News* of 30 May 1944 reminds readers of 'Japan's Lofty Spirit':

In sharp contrast to the wanton ruthlessness of British and American armed forces is the scrupulous regard which the Imperial Japanese troops display... for the preservation of historical monuments even though the place where they are situated may be of strategic importance.

A Public Library at 35 Garden Road

Of particular interest is that fact that a Public Library was to be opened in Hong Kong and 'after months of careful preparation' an advertisement for staff was in the newspaper on 31 May, as the opening was 'expected shortly'. By 28 June another article stated that capable staff had been selected and an appeal was made for donations of reading materials, with the promise that donors' names would be attached to books. The 'Preparatory Committee' was located in the Education Department. By 2 July the first 77 books had been received and on the 13th the site of the library was announced:

The former Helena May Institute in Garden Road has been decided on as the premises... the opening date has, however, not yet been fixed. An inspection of the site was made by a number of Government officials recently.

An official notice was placed in the newspaper on 5 July by the Government stipulating the rules and regulations for the library. 'Ordinary' readers were those aged 14 and above, whereas those between ages 8 and 14 were 'Minor' readers. There was also a category of 'Special' readers, who would be given passes for the special sections (though what these were is not mentioned.) Potential readers were instructed how to use the library and these were some of the rules:

5. Readers must fill in the titles of the books which he wishes to read on a form and submit same together with the Reading Permit, to the official in charge in exchange for a Seating Permit.

7. Books and the Seating Permit must be returned to the official in charge after reading when the Reading Permit will be returned.

8. Readers wishing to select their own books or literature may obtain permission from the official in charge and, if approved, they may be given Seating Permits and their respective Reading Permits collected.

9. The titles of the books borrowed by the above mentioned readers must be reported to the official in charge.

Donations were still being welcomed on 12 August, by which time over 4,000 Japanese books had been catalogued and thousands more were still to be processed. 'It is understood that the library will be in three sections, with books and publications in Japanese, Chinese and English available for readers.'

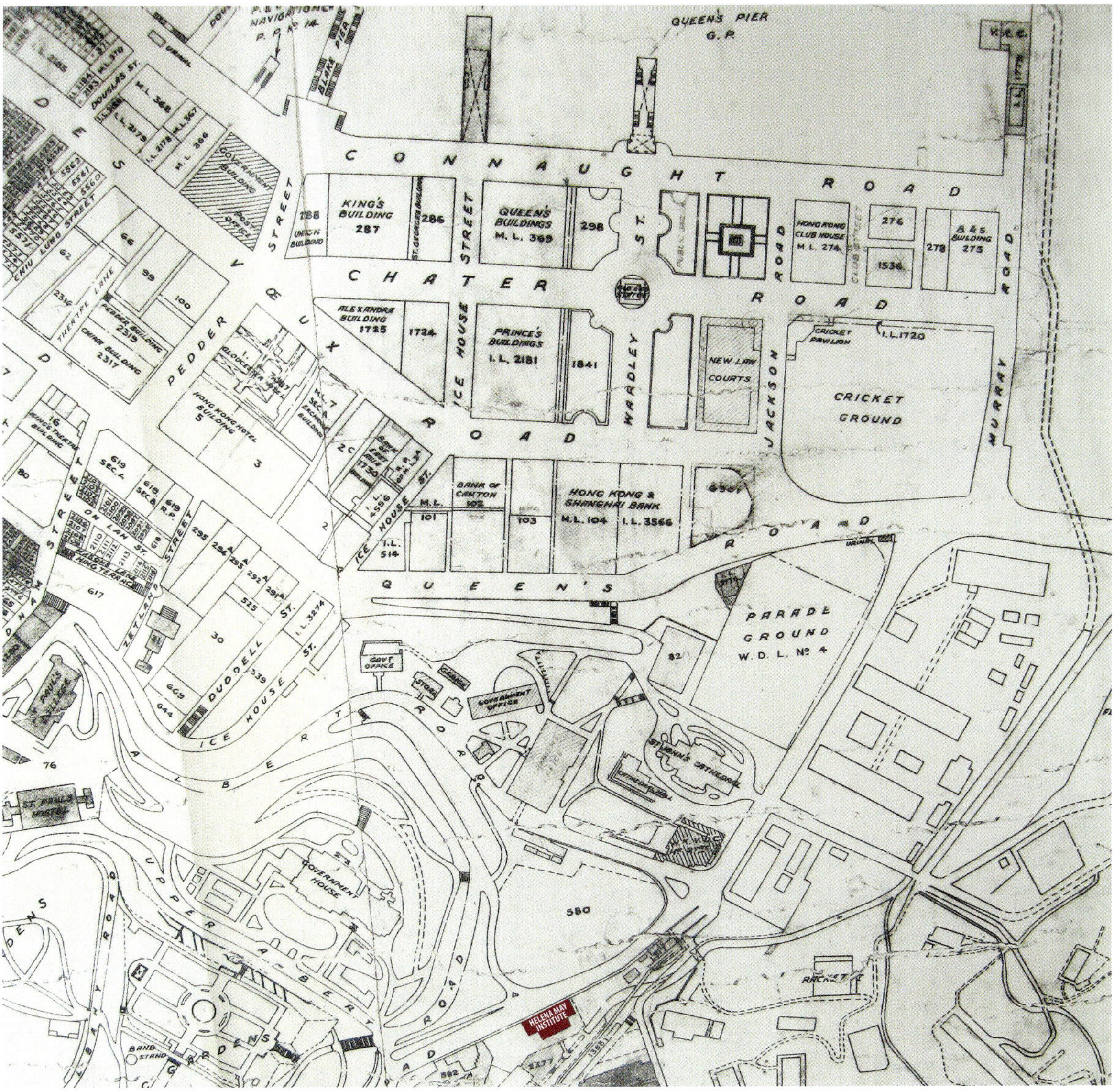

Central district, 1936

The next mention of the library in the newspaper was on 5 October, which gave an estimated opening date – the middle of November. By now over 40,000 books had been collected, and there was also to be a newspaper section with the latest local and foreign journals. Further:

An innovation of the new Library will be a special Children's Room, with accommodations for 40, which will be stocked with publications of interest to juveniles. Another new feature will be the smoking room for smoker-patrons of the Library.

An item on 1 November noted that the contemplated opening of the public library 'to improve cultural conditions in Hong Kong' and to 'extend and promote Oriental culture amongst the people here' had already served to revive interest in Chinese art as evidenced by large attendances at exhibitions of paintings and calligraphy. There is great praise for Chinese people and their culture and condemnation of Anglo-American influences. The current war is deemed to be about both 'emancipation' and 'ideology'.

On 8 November it is announced:

Alterations to the former Helena May Institute in Garden Road will be completed this week so that the opening of the Hong Kong Public library at this site is expected to take place on or about November 20. A large number of books and literature has already been received from various sources …Further donations …will be gratefully accepted.

However, November passed and the library was still not open. It was not until the 30th that the official opening date could be announced, along with details of the hours of operation, which were to be 9.30am to 7.30pm Monday to Saturday and 9.30am to 4.30pm on Sunday:

High Government officials, as well as representatives of the various cultural organizations in Hongkong, have been invited to attend the opening of the Hongkong Public Library in Garden Road on December 5, as preparations have almost been completed by Mr Kanda, the Librarian.

Anti-Japanese books had been securely locked away 'after cataloguing had brought them to light' and 'the reading tables and chairs and newspaper racks were all from the University.'[43]

Wednesday 6 December: 'Public Library Officially Opened by His Excellency the Governor' is the front page news. It was now claimed that there were nearly 400,000 volumes: 354,749 in the Main Library, of which 135,275 came from the former Hongkong University Library, another 45,244 from the Chinese section, and 174,230 from the Fung Ping Shan Library. Most of these were reference and technical books. Another 14,932 volumes dealt with art, literature, culture, history, etc. (sic) and of these 2,892 were for children aged five to six years and 5,408 for younger children.

On entering the Library there is a newspaper reading room on the left of the entrance, with the various reading matter being housed in the main room. There are two rooms set apart for children between five and six years of age on the next floor, with another room for children under four years of age. The office staff are also located on this floor. The total number of people making use of the library at one time has been limited to 85.

The *Hong Kong News* on Saturday 16 December 1944 proclaimed a celebration of the third anniversary of Hongkong's surrender on 25 December. There was to be a varied programme specially arranged by the authorities for the occasion. 'Government offices, public and private concerns as well as local schools will be closed on that day so that one and all may join in the celebrations.'

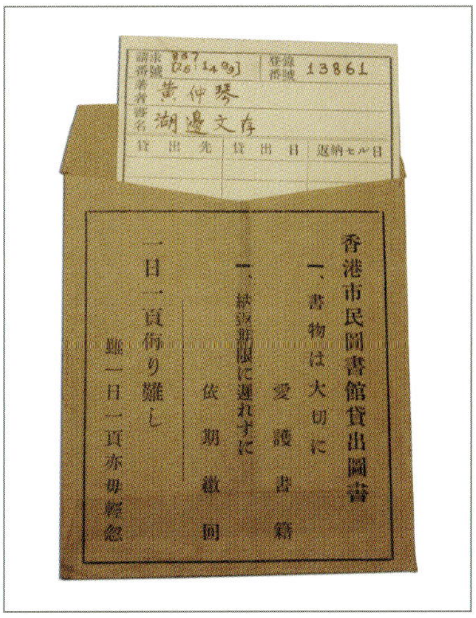

Book pocket from the Japanese Public Library

There were no more anniversary celebrations. On 6 August 1945 the Americans dropped an atomic bomb on Hiroshima, and another was dropped on Nagasaki on the 9th. On the 14th Emperor Hirohito announced Japan's unconditional surrender. Soon after the senior British officer, Franklin Gimson, who had been in Stanley camp, took over as officer administering the Government and British sovereignty of the colony was reclaimed. Rear Admiral Sir Cecil Harcourt arrived on 30 August with units of the British Pacific Fleet to establish a temporary military government. The Japanese surrender in Hong Kong was formally accepted in Government House on 16 September.

ENDNOTES

1 *South China Morning Post*, 25 November, 1916
2 *Administrative Report 1916*, p.22
3 *Administrative Report 1916*, Section XI General Observations, p.27
4 Diary excerpts courtesy of Veronica Johnston, youngest daughter of Iris
5 Personal communication from Marjorie Bray to Esther Morris July 2006
6 *Hong Kong Government Gazette* of 17 April 1919
7 *South China Morning Post*,11 September 1919
8 *South China Morning Post*,18 September 1919
9 A Short History of the Helena May Institute, 1934 reprinted in 1979, p.14
10 www3.shropshire-cc.gov.uk/benson.htm
11 Roberts, 1939, p.84
12 http://sunzi1.lib.hku.hk/hkgro/view/s1921/2267.pdf
13 Gillingham, 1983, p.109
14 *A Short History of the Helena May Institute*, 1934 reprinted in 1979, p.14-15
15 *South China Morning Post*,22 June 1922
16 *South China Morning Post*,19 August 1922
17 Angus, 1985, various pages
18 *A Short History of the Helena May Institute*, 1934 reprinted in 1979, p.15
19 Personal communication to the Helena May on 13 February 2003
20 Roberts, 1939, p.239
21 Benson, 1978
22 Lethbridge, 1978, p.12
23 Benson, 1931, p.7
24 Benson, 1978, 30th June 1931
25 Roberts, 1939, p.252
26 http://sunzi1.lib.hku.hk/hkgro/view/s1931/2380.pdf
27 Spurr, 1995, p.153
28 Fung Chi Ming, 2005
29 Hosford, 2002, p.112-114
30 Gillingham ,1983, p.110
31 Information supplied by their granddaughter – Sue Gemmell
32 *Report of the Director of Public Works for the Year 1937*
33 Appendix I, p.13
34 Personal communication to Esther Morris July 2006
35 Gittens, 1969
36 Tsang, 2004, p.121
37 Leiper, 1982, p.75 and p.82
38 Leiper, 1982, p.80
39 Harrop
40 Tsang, 2004, p.126
41 HongKong News, 15 April 1942
42 Tsang, 2004, p.127
43 Mellor, 1980, Vol. 1, p.100

THE
HELENA
MAY

THIS ANNEXE WAS BUILT
WITH FUNDS DONATED BY
THE HONGKONG JOCKEY CLUB
AND WAS OPENED BY
LADY BLACK
ON THE 13TH MARCH 1958

PLEASE
RING

送信人等
在此候音
非請勿准

THE HELENA MAY INSTITUTE
梅夫人婦女會
TRADESMEN'S ENTRANCE
ONLY
只准商人入內

Deliveries:
Please press the bell
貨物送遞 請按門鈴

4. *Post Second World War to the End of the Cultural Revolution*

Assigned to the Helena May Institute, the Royal Air Force collected the books of the Citizen's Library into one room and placed it under the University's control. Sloss (the Vice-Chancellor) offered them the use of the books; this they accepted but refused his offer to sell them the 2,200 books that comprised the Jordan Memorial Library, by then badly infested with worm and eaten by cockroaches, at 2/6d a volume.[1]

* * *

At the liberation of the Colony, Mr John Fleming of Messrs. Lowe, Bingham and Matthews, visited the Institute as soon as he could get in from Stanley Internment Camp. On September 6th 1945, while still in camp, Mrs Black, the President of the Helena May, had signed a letter in company with Mrs Dunlop, chairman of the House Committee, authorising Messrs. Lowe, Bingham and Matthews to act as Trustees of the Institute for the time being. With the arrival of British forces the building was immediately requisitioned by the R.A.F. as Headquarters, and Mr Fleming was able to act as Trustee for the Institute in this matter. Fortunately the deeds and lease were in the custody of the bank and had escaped destruction.

The building had been entirely stripped of furniture and fittings during the Japanese occupation, and the original extensive Library was completely lost or dispersed. The sole possessions of the Helena May which remained on our premises were the two fine blackwood seats which still stood in the entrance hall. In view of the wholesale looting that had taken place this was quite remarkable.[2]

Civil government was formally restored in Hong Kong on 1 May 1946, when Sir Mark Young resumed his interrupted governorship. Jean Gittens, daughter of Sir Robert Ho Tung, sailed back to Hong Kong from Melbourne with about 30 other passengers, and a number of race horses, in August.[3] Arriving on the 18th the first news to greet them was that Star Ferry workers were on strike. They found that many homes had been looted, but reunions more than made up for that - Jean saw her father for the first time in five years. She notes that the harbour was 'seemingly untouched by the ravages of war' and the tram to the Peak was running again, but 'the devastation of this once exclusive residential district was pathetic.'

All of the bronze statues had gone from Statue Square, and there were few cars left. A Thanksgiving service was held on 1 September in St John's Cathedral to mark the first anniversary of Liberation Day, although the stained glass windows were still missing and the organ had not yet been restored. However, Jean comments that in a remarkably short time the city had become 'a model of law and order with all its services functioning... had once again established itself as one of the busiest centres of the world trade' Cathay Pacific had taken to the skies, electricity supplies were functioning and there was even air-conditioning in picture theatres. However, thousands of people were coming back from China and the housing situation was desperate.

Early in 1946 accommodation for working women was very much in demand for many had been brought back by their firms for essential work in the Colony. They were living in very crowded conditions in the few hotels and boarding houses open to civilians at that time. The Trustees were extremely anxious to meet this demand by reopening the Helena May for these women, but apart from the fact that the R.A.F. could not vacate the building until other quarters were found, there were serious legal difficulties to be surmounted as well.[4]

While waiting for the building to be vacated an ad hoc committee of ladies interested in the reopening of the Institute had been formed.

They had been busy placing orders for furniture, linen, cutlery, kitchen equipment and other necessities. The R.A.F. very kindly allowed a representative of this committee to inspect the building in company with a contractor so that on de-requisition work was started on the interior without delay. A number of the old staff of servants had returned including the No. 1 Boy. Some were put on a retaining fee to enable them to live until such time as their services should be required.[5]

The Building de-requisitioned

The building was finally de-requisitioned 'after many false hopes' on 8 December 1946. When the R.A.F. left there was a meeting of Council Members Designate at the offices of Messrs Lowe, Bingham and Matthews on 19 December. Lady Young was proposed and seconded as prospective President of the Council and took the chair. The building was accorded its nominal pre-war value of $169,730. Temporary dormitory rooms were to be provided on the ground floor. Mr Fleming suggested that the Library room might temporarily be used as a bedroom because of 'the present stringency of any accommodation in the Colony'. Priority was to be given to the 'Working Woman' described in the original Constitution, where it was the intention particularly to care for girls from abroad.

HELENA MAY TO BE INCORPORATED AGAIN

An Ordinance to provide for the incorporation of the council of the Helena May Institute for Women and for the vesting in the corporation the property and rights of the Association known as the Helena May Institute for Women is to be placed before the Legislative Council.

There would be an entrance fee or re-registration fee of $15 to be paid by all members, and a monthly subscription of $3. The pre-war 'No 1 boy' (caterer and steward), Ho Yum Chuen, reported for duty and undertook to recruit a complete staff. Mr Fleming also reported that he had retained Miss Margery Matheson 'who had wide experience in hotel management in the Colony' as Manageress.

On 5 January 1947 the *Hong Kong Sunday Herald* had the headline 'Helena May to be Incorporated Again'. A draft Bill was published in the *Government Gazette*, along with the constitution of the Institute, to be placed before the Legislative Council.

The object of the corporation shall be to provide for the welfare of women and girls of the Colony. There are to be resident members (boarders) and subscriber members. One black ball in five will exclude.

The originally incorporated 'company' had 16 shareholders and a person ceased to be a shareholder if absent from the Colony for more than a year. Owing to the war, the evacuation of some women, and repatriation of many of those who had been interned, there were no longer any shareholders. Further, the Memorandum and Articles of Association had no provision for such circumstances, and so the 'company' effectively could not function.

The Helena May Institute for Women Ordinance of 1946 detailed in the Constitution the composition of the Council. It was to have 15 members allocated across specific categories:

- Eight subscriber members who were British subjects of European race
- Two subscriber members of European race, but not British subjects
- Two subscriber members of Chinese race
- Three residential members

The Helena May Returns to Life

The Institute at this time was vested in a Council composed of Lady Young, Mrs Mary Campbell, Mrs Margery Cassidy, Mrs Margery Everett, Mrs Katherine Fleming, Mrs Edith Rowell, Mrs Mabel Annett, Mrs Ivy Sykes, Mrs Elsie Dunbar, Mrs Marlis Gundersen, Mrs Victoria Lo (daughter of Robert Ho Tung) and Mrs Dorothy Woo.

According to other reports on the same day, the YWCA was up and running again with Mrs Beth Wright as secretary for the English-speaking membership, many American missionaries had arrived in Hong Kong, and the Lee Theatre was showing the film *The Bride Came C.O.D.* with Bette Davis and James Cagney.

It was noted in the Council meeting on 7 January that the RAF had not paid any rent since October – a sum of $6,538. But there were other matters for the hatted and gloved ladies to deal with. Miss Matheson's salary was to be $300 per month, the cost of furnishing the dormitory would be $1,000 and a carpenter had been employed at $12 per day. Enquiries were to be made

regarding hire or purchase of a piano and it was thought that it would be an advantage to have French books in the Library.

At the Legislative Council meeting of 16 January the Hon. Mr M. M. Watson moved the second reading of the Helena May Institute for Women Bill:

An Ordinance to provide for the incorporation of the Council of the Helena May Institute for Women and for vesting in the Corporation the property and rights of the Association...

Discussions had taken place with the Hon. Mr T. M. Hazlerigg CBE, MC, a member of the Legislative Council who was acting on behalf of the Government, regarding the manner in which the activities of the Institute could be revived. This gentleman thought it might look ungracious on the part of the Government if it 'suddenly descended on the Institution and adopted it as its own without any reference to those who had in the past run the Institute'. A cable was sent to Mrs Black, the former President, who was then in England, and she was asked to get in touch with seven other Council members (eight being a quorum) to obtain their consent to the Government's suggestion of reconstituting the Institute.

The former Articles of the Association were very much out of date and contained many contradictory provisions - possibly due to the fact that they had been altered time after time without any references being made to other parts of the Ordinance. Mr Hazlerigg suggested that the constitution should be included as part of the whole in the schedule, and Mr Watson said he agreed with the proposal which accordingly was adopted. As a result the new constitution was clear, modern and intended to prevent any legal trouble arising in the future. The tradition of the wife of the Governor of the Colony being involved with the Institute, following the original connection with Lady May, would be continued, as Lady Young had consented to be one of the members of the new Council. The Hon. Mr Hazlerigg seconded, and the Bill was given its second and third readings and passed into law.

At this momentous time the Swatow Lace Company in Pedder Street was advertising its Chinese New Year sale. 'Popular' bed sheets could be bought for $19.50 per piece and a silk embroidered lady's slip for $7.95. Bernard Shaw's 'mighty spectacle' *Caesar and Cleopatra* in 'Technicolor' starring Vivien Leigh and Claude Rains was coming soon.

The Institute re-opened on 18 January 1947 with new residents and within the next few weeks many old members rejoined and brought with them new members. In mid-February an 'At Home' day was held to celebrate the re-opening and according to a newspaper report[6] it was hoped that the pre-war amenities would be renewed, as the Institute 'was extensively used not only as a hostel but as a social centre for lectures, concerts and dancing classes.'

In March a tennis net was purchased and posts put up. Lady Young resigned as Chairman in April but remained on the Council. There were to be ten tables of bridge and mahjong one afternoon, with the profits going to the Library, which now had 500 books. The following month the companies in which the Helena May held shares were listed. By now there was a long waiting list for rooms and to cope with demand, two of the public rooms off the Lounge – previously the Reading Room and Drawing Room – were turned into sleeping quarters. The five years of neglect had taken its toll and income was needed to cover the high expenditure on repairs and furnishings. However, by the summer the Institute was firmly on its feet again.

The Institute will always bear a debt of gratitude to the friends who in those days of reorganization gave so much of their time and labour to get the Institute back to its pre-war basis. At a period of short supply, firms and private individuals gave unstinted help in procuring all those necessities essential to the equipping of such a large establishment as the Helena May. It is due entirely to the efforts of all those friends who have contributed so much in time and labour that the Helena May has been able to resume again the work in Hong Kong so much desired of its original founders.[7]

Long time member Dorothy Collins, who died in 2003, came to Hong Kong in 1947 with her husband, who was in the Colonial Service. She remembered that food was so plentiful that they were sending parcels and material home to England, where there was still rationing. People were in great demand and girls were being 'imported' from England as secretaries and coming to live at the Helena May. Dorothy recalled that the place was full of young women. The Library was being reassembled, with the wife of the Director of Education, Mrs Edith Rowell, in charge. There were balls in midsummer and at Christmas, and she said that everyone who joined the Helena May was very fond of it.[8]

In September Mrs Howell (Carol Bateman), who had been interned in Stanley during the war and whose husband owned a sawmill in the New Territories, was anxious to start children's dancing classes, which she had done previously in Shanghai. From the following month there were four sessions a week, at a charge of $20 for the room hire. The Reel Club started their weekly practices on Monday evenings from 5.30pm to 7.00pm at $300 for 24 practices. By the time of the AGM on the 30th all the old staff had returned and there were now 38 residents and 300 members.

The Council reported in November that the number of books in the Library would grow from 780 to over 1100 during the next few weeks, and the Hong Kong Council of Women's suggestion that the Helena May should become an affiliated member was agreed upon. It was noted in the December Council Minutes that 'the police had applied for the return of the rifle, but as a shot gun in replacement would cost $250 it was decided that the watchman should be provided with a baton.'

The writer Shirley Hazzard was in Hong Kong around this time with her parents. In her award winning novel, *The Great Fire*, set around 1947, Peter Exley, a close friend of the main character, finds himself working in the bank building (the tallest building in those days at 12 storeys) with 'three servicewomen... Brenda, Monica and Norah... none of them pretty, none really young' who lived at 'the Helena May Hostel above the town'. They invite Peter there for tea for his birthday, where they sit in the 'lofty lounge' on a 'wicker settee' which has 'plumped-down cushions' covered with 'chintz roses'. The 'thick-bodied women' go 'stumping off to fetch cake and a bowl of sugar with silver tongs' and are 'fondling' the dog belonging to the 'maiden directress'. Shirley had remembered these details from her own visits to the Helena May as a young woman.[9]

The Institute is also mentioned in Han Suyin's book *A Many Splendoured Thing*, set during the period September 1949 to February 1950:

'Nice looking girl, Miss Kilton' volunteered Martha. 'She used to stay at the Helena May. But I was looking up the list of girls there yesterday and she'd moved out.'

Then later in the book, when she was looking for accommodation with her daughter:

The Chinese YWCA was crowded, and children were not admitted. The Helena May Institute and the European YWCA were for whites. Everything else was too expensive; the rent of a small room was as much as my month's salary.

Communist takeover in China

1949 saw the end of the civil war in China and the Communist takeover, with Mao Tse-tung becoming Chairman of the People's Republic of China. It was an anxious time in Hong Kong with refugees flooding over the border – sometimes as many as ten thousand in one week. It was also the year in which many of those who had been evacuated to Australia returned to Hong Kong from Sydney on the "Hwa Lien", an old inter-island New Zealand ferry. One person, who became a long term resident of the Helena May, was Phil Kirby 'a gorgeous glamorous woman'. Another was Norma (Stevens) Thompson, who remembers attending Carol Bateman's classes after school. Her mother was a member who used the library. Norma recalls dancing 'a la Isadora Duncan' along with Susan Strellet and Patricia Wickerson in bare feet in white tunics 'the exercise was great... leaps and bounds and graceful movements...no chomped up toes as the ballet dancers endured'. Later they did ballroom dancing and tap-dancing. 'Carol was a special woman', who helped Norma to overcome her shyness.[10]

The big news in the August Council meeting was the installation of a radio set in the lounge:

ReDiffusion (sic) has now been installed and a notice is to be placed on, or mear (sic), the receiving set reminding listerners (sic) to switch off when they leave the lounge.

The spelling mistakes serve to remind us that Minutes were being typed without the benefits of word processing programmes! However, there were weightier issues being discussed as well. The Helena May Institute had two representatives on the Hong Kong Council of Women and resolutions for a forthcoming meeting were concerned with: the lack of sufficient hostel accommodation for working women and girls at a cost they could afford; the need for the Government to make fuller use of the services of women on committees 'in order that feminine opinion be given a chance to add its weight to public affairs'; and the desire for equal pay for equal work 'regardless of sex'.

The AGM at the Helena May in October reported that the library had over 2,100 books, and the Institute was grateful to the Jockey Club for its donation of $5,000, half of which was being given to the Library and half was being spent making the lounge and residents' sitting room more comfortable.

It was in this year that Marjorie Bottomley became a member of the Helena May – being sponsored by her mother, who had been a member since 1929. Marjorie was born in Hong Kong, but had been overseas for her education and had gone to school with two of Helena May's granddaughters – Margaret (Whitworth) Osmaston and Felicity Johnston. In 1952 she married Denis Bray, who was also born in Hong Kong and returned after being educated in Britain. During his career in Government from the age of 25 Denis rose to the rank of Secretary for Home Affairs and on occasion acted as Chief Secretary and as Governor. He was also an Associate Member of the Helena May.

Hong Kong a Haven of Stability

In August 1950 Jean Gittens broadcast the true situation in Hong Kong on Australian national radio - noting that she found the place to be 'normal and stable in everyday living (though) Government policy relative to its neighbours tended towards an altruism which, to some extent, was against the interests of her own citizens... Hong Kong had become a haven for all who found living conditions untenable elsewhere.'[11] Helena's daughters sent out from England a photographic portrait of their mother, to take the place of the oil painting of her which previously had hung in the Lounge, but was lost during the Japanese occupation. The chimneys were cleaned by the HongKong and Shanghai Banking Corporation sweep in December, and the Institute became a centre for the distribution of wool for the knitting of 'comforts' (socks, mufflers and mittens) for the Forces in Korea.

The population swelled from half a million in August 1945 to around two million by the 1951 census. Rosemary Read[12] moved into the Helena May in 1951 for a period of about eight months, as she had a very good job with Shell and was reluctant to go on leave with her family. Rosemary was born in Hong Kong in 1932, and her ancestors had first come to the Far East more than a century ago. A Cantonese speaker, at the age of eight she was evacuated to Australia along with around 2000 other people. Her family returned to the colony in 1949, and as she had taken a short secretarial course she was immediately employed by the government at $380 a month as a 'beginner'. Her skills were in great demand at this time and five months of intensive practice on her 13 hapless bosses brought a more lucrative offer from the Asiatic Petroleum Company (Shell).

She remembers sharing the first floor north corner room on the Garden Road side of the building with Elizabeth (Tommy) Wiseman, who worked for the American consulate across the road. Theirs was one of the permanent double rooms:

it cost a little more than a dormitory and they tried to match up friends for harmony's sake. That is why I waited a month to get in, Tommy played hockey too so we were friends and when her roommate left she asked on my behalf. No-one in the dorms wanted it, or probably didn't want to pay the extra. The transients were in two four-bed dormitories on the ground floor, windows opening to Garden Road, now part of the "public" area. I was considered "long-term" enough to qualify for the twin-room. Single rooms had very long waiting lists.

The single rooms, for more permanent residents, were on the Peak Tram side. One of the occupants in her mid-twenties, who had a room on the top floor, apparently liked to dance around in the nude to entertain the students at night school in St Joseph's College opposite.

Miss Matheson, the Manageress, is remembered as being strict, but kind, and definitely not an ogre. There were about 20 residents there at this time, some of whom worked for the Government or the Bank and were waiting to be allocated quarters. The others were older than Tommy and Rosemary, and she remembers them all being very helpful to each other, though the older ladies would complain if the younger ones made too much noise. One of the residents 'who was very kind to new chums' was Muriel Parsons. She was a schoolteacher already in her 30s. In the evenings they would read or sew or play bridge, and sometimes there would be a cocktail party – to which everyone was invited. Rosemary does not remember any outside functions but she has very fond memories of the Christmas party, which was organised by the senior residents. The place was beautifully decorated with Christmas trees and flowers from Lee Wing Kee, and residents could invite friends to the lunch.

Rosemary paid $250 a month for her shared room and $25 a month to her amah. Residents could sign friends in for lunch and dinner and could eat very well for $7.50, which suited Rosemary's boyfriend Desmond Inglis, who at that time was a junior clerk with Jardines. (In 1955, although he had worked there for seven years, he had to leave so that they could marry.) The girls found that they could stay out quite late if they tipped $10 each month to the Night Watchman, whom they called "Bruiser" because of his stocky build. 'We also tipped So Hoi, our particular "houseboy" who would bring a sandwich and tea to the room if you came in too late for dinner. It kept things moving along happily. So Hoi was quite a talented painter and most of the girls at the time bought one of his paintings. He signed them "So Hi". I paid $80 for mine'.

One resident had to wait six months to marry her beau – a lieutenant in the army. They spent a great deal of time sitting on the railings outside the building, even when it was raining, and thus earned the nicknames 'Drip' and 'Drop'. It was not unusual for several young men to be waiting outside the dormitories on the ground floor trying to catch sight of the girls inside. Joan Forrest, a Canadian lady in her late twenties who also worked for Shell, had the single room next to Tommy & Rosemary. They had to keep an eye on her as she was and rather more venturesome – 'our local femme fatale' – rumour had it that she once tried to sneak her boyfriend in via the fire escape. Eventually 'her old Canadian flame appeared in Hong Kong with an engagement ring and of course took exception to her circle of admirers!' Rosemary comments:

I think we were all more tolerant and good-natured to each other, the staff, our Manageress (and I never saw any of the committee officially anyway, they were on the same level as the Jardine's and Hong Kong Bank hierarchy, one did not reason why etc.) than perhaps some of the later residents might have been.[13]

The May 1951 Council Minutes report the recurrence of stone throwing, which had resulted in a large pane of glass being broken. 'The culprits were thought to be servicemen'. Presumably they were trying to catch the attention of the girls inside rather being mere vandals. On a more positive note, the following month it was reported that Lady Grantham (wife of the Governor

Top from left: Peter & Margaret Gilson (Drip & Drop), Desmond Inglis, Joan (Franklin) Izard
Middle from left: Joan Forrest, Rosemary (Read) Inglis, Centre front: Elizabeth (Tommy) Wiseman

and Patron) had visited and a supply of fresh vegetables was being sent regularly from the Government house garden, which was much appreciated.

By July the young 'makee-learn' wash amah's wages had been increased from $75 to $85, and in September it was proposed that the Night Watchman's wages be increased from $90 to $105 but to earn this 'in future he will be responsible for washing up the crockery used in the lounge during the mornings'. The October Minutes include a plea from the residents' representative, Miss Ormiston – a long term resident – asking if anything could be done about the early morning noises made by learner drivers 'coming down and backing up the steep slip road opposite the building.' How different Hong Kong was then.

In March 1953 it was noted that $231 had been collected from members and the money very fairly distributed by the No. 1 boy for the Chinese New Year 'cumshaw'. Miss Bateman wished to hire the hall for an additional dancing class, but the Committee decided that her request could not be met, as otherwise no free afternoon would be available for letting the Hall for entertainments in which Members of the Helena May could benefit. After a thorough inspection of the grounds in May, a Mr Dean recommended the construction of a number of raised retaining beds to check the constant washing away of soil due to heavy rain, as it was feared that damage might eventually be done to the foundations of the building. The Council agreed to the sum of $304 being spent on raised beds and the transferring of some of the soil from the vegetable garden. Lady Young, who had become Chairman of the House Committee the previous year, was going to find out what the additional cost would be to erect a fence in front of the laundry drying court, as 'at present the laundry hangs on the line unashamed in full view of the Club, and it is not an attractive sight.'

Besides being concerned with internal matters, the Institute helped another charitable group by allowing the Salvation Army to display and sell embroidered work one day a month. In the July Council meeting items discussed included an extension to the Library, a new

The laundry in the garden and St Joseph's College opposite

dormitory for the male staff, plus additional showers and toilets, and a wash-room for the amahs. There was a long waiting list for accommodation and the building of an Annexe was being considered. There was some discussion on the subject of allowing bachelors to join under the new arrangements, but the majority of the Council thought that Associate Membership should be kept to relatives of regular members, and the proposal for bachelor membership was rejected. In August history was made with a Dr Griffiths joining the Library as the first Associate Member. Presumably his wife was a member already. The Library premises were enlarged and the number of books in circulation had swelled to in excess of 12,000. This included a substantial children's section, which was found to be well patronised.[14]

An 'unpleasant incident' was reported by Mrs Gwen Faber in April 1954. Two young American men gained entry into the Helena May through the pantry after the front door was closed at 10.30pm and insisted on trying to go into the North dormitory via the wash room. They were enquiring after one of the young resident members and refused to accept the assurance that she was out to dinner. These young men were eventually persuaded to leave the premises, but not before they had intimidated the Night Watchman and offered offhand insults to Miss Matheson, who had been called down to cope with the situation. These young men were requested to return at an early date to apologise for their behaviour. The young resident member concerned was spoken to and after a lapse of some days the young men returned and apologised – but did not disclose their names.

In the same month a thief gained access in the early hours and stole a sum of money and jewellery from Room 12, occupied by a Miss Dunn. A resident member on the way to her bath at 6am thought she saw a man crouching in the corridor, but did not raise any alarm, or even report her suspicion until lunchtime, when the burglary was discovered.

At the September Council meeting it was reported that Miss Carol Bateman did not use the Hall for her dancing classes from 21 to 30 August as she was using the Empire Theatre to rehearse the stage show she produced annually in aid of charity. Members were also told that 'on a few occasions recently men selling merchandise have been found wandering around the bedroom floors. Resident members expecting tailors to arrive for dress fittings have been asked to notify the No. 1 boy of their arrangements'. By October, the system whereby a coolie sold soft drinks from a tub in the Hall during dancing classes had proved to be a success, and children had ceased running up and down stairs to collect their refreshments.

The AGM on 21 October reported that the Hall had been rented regularly by Carol Bateman for dancing classes and during the winter season weekly by the

Reel Club. It was also used for the showing of films and children's parties. Most importantly:

Our great achievement and major item of expense this year is the completion of the building of an extension to the Library with the servants' quarters below it which cost just over $24,000. Our residential accommodation continues to be full and we have our usual long waiting list. The Council is seriously considering the possibility of building an Annexe, as we feel that the need for accommodation at a moderate price, for working women, will always be felt in Hong Kong, and now that the YWCA has closed down, this need is more acute than ever. In view of the financial position of the Helena May Institute for Women and the need for more accommodation for Residents, Mr Faber put forth the suggestion of building an Annexe for maybe 12 or 16, preferably single rooms. A new plan of the property has been prepared by Mr S. E. Faber A.F.C. and was produced for Council Members to see. This has clearly been marked which is garden ground and which is building ground. This project is to be discussed more fully.

The November Council Meeting Minutes note that Miss Bateman held two dancing displays during the month, which were in association with the Festival of Arts. In connection with the proposed new extension, Mesdames Faber, Sykes and Bowring had visited Mr Stewart of the Hongkong & Shanghai Bank to discussion the possibility of the Bank advancing a loan to help finance the proposed Annexe. He advised the amount they were prepared to advance against the Helena May's security, and should an additional loan be required he felt that the Bank would give most sympathetic consideration to the matter.

After a general discussion by the Council tentative proposals were agreed upon. The Annexe should contain: not less than 16 single rooms, each with wash basin; one dormitory containing 3 or 4 beds, in cubicles with 2 wash basins; two storage rooms – one for general storage and one for trunks; one pantry with small servants' room adjoining; one room for amahs containing wash basin & hanging lines for laundry; one room containing 3 baths and 6 showers, in cubicles; and four separate lavatories. The present dormitories would eventually revert to their original purpose as sitting and reading rooms. These could prove a source of income to the Helena May if hired out for wedding receptions, bridge teas or cocktail parties.

The film *Love is a Many Splendoured Thing*, starring William Holden and Jennifer Jones, was made in 1955. Joan Campbell, aged 24, had arrived in Hong Kong to teach ballet with Carol Bateman and came to live at the Helena May. She remembers[15] at that time the population of the colony being around one million; Conduit Road was a country road, and Garden Road was a two

Carol Bateman, 1967

way thoroughfare and you could park a car right outside the building. The Blue Room was used as a dormitory shared by four girls, each with a single bed in different corners of the room and dressing tables in the middle. Joan initially had to share here until a room became available upstairs. The amahs were all female and there was one who cleaned and washed and ironed clothes for every three or four people. The residents paid the amahs directly. The main staff members were generally older men, who had limited English but were always very kind and courteous.

At this time, the present Green Room housed the Library. The main room was a sitting room with many large comfortable rattan armchairs and sofas and low tables. The upholstery was very English with lots of floral coverings. The atmosphere was extremely welcoming and cosy and the room was nearly always full. With no television as a distraction, it was very sociable with people talking or playing cards. Dinner and breakfast were served in the room downstairs, and then the tables and chairs were cleared away for the ballet classes that Joan taught with Carol Bateman. Lunch would just be light snacks served in the lounge upstairs.

Joan remembers that it was easier to mix with people in higher positions and so she went to 'wonderful' garden parties at Government House. Residents also often received invitations from visiting ships to attend their dances. At weekends she and friends would sometimes have a barbeque out in the garden – sitting on the grass – and there was an annual residents' party.

Another resident in 1955 was Joan Franklin (later Izard) who came to stay after her father, P. F. Franklin, died at the beginning of the year. He had risen to be General Manager of the *South China Morning Post* after having spent nearly four years in camps during the Japanese occupation. Joan has earlier memories of her mother, who was a member of the Helena May, using the 'excellent' library and the two of them having afternoon tea there. She worked for Lowe, Bingham and Matthews during the eight months she was in the Helena May and then moved into Hong Kong Bank quarters. She stayed in the dormitory on the corner of the building beside Garden Road 'where people complained the buses used to change gear noisily and wake them up, but they never bothered me'. There were four beds there and the two other girls occupying the room at the time were Eileen Wade and a German girl called Helga. One of the girls in the other dormitory was Helen (Smith) Potts, who came from Perth in Western Australia. Her father-in-law to be, Alec Potts, was a Jockey Club Steward. Joan remembers:

We all got on very well indeed and I loved everything about the Helena May, including the food, which some people (amazingly to me) used to complain about. On Sundays, as a special treat because we were in a dormitory, we were given breakfast in bed, bacon and eggs, toast and marmalade and tea, all on a huge tray. I shared a *table in the dining room with Joan Campbell, who astonished me as she had her own tin of "Bemax" which she would sprinkle on her breakfast cereal. Being out of my mother's care for the first time went to my head a bit, and I was out every night beyond the "curfew". The big front doors would be locked, and you had to ring a bell to be let in a side door by a surly "boy". After 3 weeks he "dobbed" me in to Miss Matheson, and she called me in to her office and told me off and threatened to tell my mother!!! Horrors!!! I have since learned that I should have tipped the boy and he would have let me off. At this point I became ill and was hospitalized in Queen Mary Hospital with Diphtheria. (Later) I returned to the Helena May at about the same time as the fourth girl in our dormitory, a lovely Australian girl named Jennifer Jordon. We were so happy to have recovered our health (she'd had dysentery) and enjoyed life at the HM greatly. One of the boys there painted HK scenes of the harbour and junks, which cost $100 and I bought one.*[16]

In April 1955, 'after a great deal of thought and planning' Mr Faber submitted plans for the new building site. He proposed that the tennis court be used, thus avoiding the necessity of cutting down trees on the first discussed site. Meanwhile, the new car park at St Joseph's Church had resulted in excess rain water flowing onto the Helena May property and it was felt that this would cause damage in due time. Help and advice was sought. In June the Jockey Club had sent their annual donation of $5000, half of which was to go to the Library, and in September a new contract had been made up by Government which changed 'Garden Lot' to 'Building Lot' for the site of the proposed new building.

The Helena May's programme of improvement and expansion to meet the demand for accommodation continued in 1956 with an overdraft of $200,000 from the Hong Kong & Shanghai Bank at a reduced rate. The project was boosted by the Stewards of the Jockey Club agreeing to an unexpected donation of $250,000 towards the building and furnishing of the Annexe. The main building was also improved to add a new cloak room, enlarge and modernise the kitchen, pantry and servants' rooms, and refurnish and decorate to a higher standard.

Joan Campbell was married in St John's Cathedral in June and held her wedding reception in the Helena May. The kitchen staff made the cake, but she remembers that she had to supply them with the pans – as she did later for her son's and daughter's wedding receptions. 'Each time the cakes were perfect.'

At the Council meeting in February 1957 it was recorded that Miss Matheson, the Manageress, was becoming less able to carry out her duties. Council members were reminded that the Helena May had been originally founded on a religious basis and it would be against Christian principles to dispense with her entirely, when morally she was the Council's responsibility.

Photographs from the ballet classes, 1-In the garden, Paula Lau (2nd from right) & Pat Stewart (at right). 2-Warm-up at the barre, Pat Stewart (at left), Grace Mak (5th from left), Michelle Gregory (at right). 3-Class given by the ballerina of a touring company which performed in Kong Kong in 1968. 4-Mrs Joan Campbell teaches a ballet class at the Carol Bateman School of Dancing, 1967.

The Annexe opens

In April the cheque for $250,000 was received from the Jockey Club, so the money for the Annexe was now available. Lady Grantham laid the cornerstone on 10 July in the area that had been the tennis court. Once the Annexe was built it was hoped that the sitting and reading rooms in the main building could prove a source of income to the Helena May if hired out for Wedding receptions, Bridge Teas or Cocktail parties. The Annexe was opened on 13 March 1958 by Lady Black, whose husband, Sir Robert, had recently been appointed Governor.

The Council Minutes for April 1960 show that a new Dining Room floor was to be laid, which would cause disruption to the dancing lessons. It was arranged with the Minister of the Union Church in Kennedy Road that their Hall could be used 'with the exception of Mondays, on which days the lessons will be held at the Helena May in the new Sitting Room'. At the September meeting Carol Bateman requested rattan armchairs for the amahs waiting, but the Council suggested 'a bench would be more suitable'.

Annelise Connell remembers her first acquaintance with the Helena May was in this year at the age of three through taking ballet lessons from Joan Campbell:

For the next 10 years, my fondest memory of the Club was the privilege of going up the enormous grand staircase to the kitchen after ballet practice and, if they were not sold out, ordering and eating three drop scones with butter. Of course, I was never allowed in the main lounge, as that was only allowed if my mother was with us.[17]

1961 was the year in which Yuri Gagarin became the first man in space and air conditioning was installed in the Helena May library, which helped to preserve the books. The census in March of that year calculates the population of Hong Kong to be 3,133,131. Typhoon Wanda on 1 September 1962 killed 131 people and made 70,000 homeless, and there was a severe drought in 1963 with water rationing as a result and only four hours of water every fourth day. The Mandarin Hotel was built on the site of Queen's Building, Martin Luther King delivered his 'I Have a Dream' Speech, Betty Friedan's *The Feminine Mystique* was published and on 22 November the President of the United States, J. F. Kennedy, was assassinated. We can only wonder at how much any of these events touched the residents and members of the Helena May. However, they would have been affected by bachelors being granted Associate Membership in this year.

It is recorded in the April 1964 Minutes that one resident had typhoid fever, and that the estimate for converting rooms 14 and 15 into a flat was $390. By July this work had been completed and a suite had been created for Mrs Gibb, the new Manageress. The terms of her contract were that she would have one afternoon off a week, preferably Thursdays, and one weekend in three. The rest of the time she would be available for the residents. The big news items at the October meeting were that 'rats had been seen in the amahs' bathroom' and there had been 'thefts of clothing from the drying ground and reports of prowlers'. The AGM reports that when the building was erected in 1916 the architect concerned estimated that it would last about 50 years. Typhoons and time had taken their toll of the fabric and now the roof was in bad condition and would have to be repaired. It must have seemed as if the prediction was correct.

In May 1965 another problem arose as damage had been caused to the Helena May building by blasting at the new Peak Tram building site. A letter was sent to those concerned. However, the main complaint of some residents was that unless they wash their hair early in the evening they cannot get it properly dry before retiring to bed. 'This may cause some difficulty as curlers etc. are not acceptable in the dining room at dinner time.' As a result it was decided to ascertain the price of two Japanese hair dryers. A question was raised in June with regard to proper attire for dinner in the dining room. It had always been the ruling that no slacks should be worn in the dining room at any time, but a few months earlier, after requests from the Residents, this ruling had been relaxed, and slacks were now permitted on any evening except Wednesdays, which was regarded as a Guest Night. In the same meeting it was agreed that a few rattan foot stools could be provided for use on the verandah as there were not enough full length chairs to go round.

During the summer Carol Bateman requested use of the Hall for three afternoons a week instead of two as at present and the Council were agreeable. Later in the year it was decided to remove the stage in the dining room as it was never used. The AGM records a waiting list of 57 for accommodation, and notes that one of the greatest problems at the Helena May was the recruitment of ladies to serve both on the Council and on Committees – a problem that probably persists in all organizations that rely on volunteers.

There was anxiety in February 1966 over the proposed Kapok Drive (subsequently renamed Cotton Tree Drive) which would pass very near to the bedrooms of the Annexe, if not over some of the roof, making some of the rooms virtually uninhabitable. The plans for Stage 2 would take part of the Botanical Gardens and grounds of Government House and involved a flyover passing the Helena May and St Joseph's Church. However, there was a great deal more to worry about over the border with the start of the Cultural Revolution. In April there were riots in Kowloon. It was the Helena May's 50th birthday year and Veronica Johnston, daughter of Iris May, was visiting at the time. She recalls:

...it was clear that the HM was then having great financial difficulties, as well as questioning its role and membership. I remember the Easter riots; I was staying in the Kowloon YMCA close to the Star Ferry terminus & saw

it all going on. My diary records that there was a strong suspicion that the proposed fare rise (in 1st class only) was being used as an excuse and that there were agitators from the mainland hard at work. I missed a City Hall concert one night because of the curfew, and had to stay another night with a distant cousin, Maura Benham, who lived on HK Island, in order to meet the historian George Endacott.[18]

In May the Crown Land Department assured the Council that Stage 2 of Kapok Drive would not be implemented for at least three years. A new Constitution had been drafted by Johnson Stokes and Master in March and the revisions were approved by the Council in May. It was also agreed that the work connected with alterations to the Servants' Chow Area should be carried out as planned. The AGM in November reports: 'The first stage of Kapok Drive is progressing all too quickly for our peace of mind...'

1967 was the year the English Schools foundation was established, and three of their schools – Glenealy, Island and Kennedy Road – were in close proximity to the Helena May, so children in their school uniforms were often seen in the Library and Main Lounge during the late afternoon. In August there were further riots by communists. Dorothy Collins remembered that people didn't know whether the Chinese would stop at the border, and that there was a lot of anti-British feeling.[19] Several residents left because of the riots and other prospective residents cancelled their bookings.[20] However, one of the 'girls' living at the Helena May during this period told Annelise Connell the following story[21]:

During this time the residents continued to take afternoon tea on the second floor balcony facing Garden Road. From this vantage point they had an excellent view of the communist protesters who went up and down Garden Road shouting slogans on their way to and from Government House. One day, a messenger was sent from the American Consulate across the road to ask if the ladies would mind stepping inside for a few minutes. They explained that they wanted to take some photos of the mob and they were concerned that if the ladies taking tea were in the picture, nobody would believe Hong Kong was on the verge of disaster with rioters wreaking havoc everywhere!

The Council also had other concerns as the retaining wall between the Helena May and the new building of the Catholic Church next door was thought to be inadequate, and damage was likely to occur to the Helena May garden in the event of heavy rain. It was decided to postpone the general redecoration of the Annexe, and agreed that separate estimates for the sewing room and pantry should be obtained. The Institute had been running at a loss for some time due to the decline in demand for rooms, and added to this the government now provided a hostel for female staff. The Auditors had advised[22] investigating every possibility for reducing expenses and a number of suggestions were put forward:

Arial view of Helena May 1963

a) Cutting out lunches completely, except for weekends and possibly a snack service.
b) Reducing staff by one baker, one cook, one coolie and several (at present redundant) amahs.
c) Reducing the laundry bill by changing sheets only once a week instead of twice.
d) Possibly abandoning outside laundry altogether and installing washing machines.
e) Reducing Library expenses.
f) Keeping all redecoration and maintenance expenses to the absolute minimum.

Times of change

Eventually it was agreed to close the Annexe from January 1968. In March a farewell party was given for Carol Bateman. She had lived at the Helena May for a short time with her daughter whilst preparing to leave. No doubt members were able to sample some of the 'excellent' cakes that the cook was producing with the recently purchased food mixer. Joan Campbell then became principal of the Carol Bateman School of Dancing.

Around 1960, Pat Stewart, now a successful local professional artist, attended Carol Bateman's dancing classes two or three times a week, starting at the age of four. In the late sixties, when her brother Alistair was a pupil at St Joseph's College, he would come down to the Helena May after school. Alistair was a talented photographer and won awards for his photography at an early age. Over a period of three to four years, starting at the age of 12, he took photos of the ballet classes, and today he still has fond memories of the hours he spent in the Helena May, doing his homework, having tea, and practising his photography while waiting for their mother to collect them both.

Rosanna Yue became Treasurer in April and continued in the position for 30 years – a great example of the loyalty of staff. However her position at that time was by no means certain, as the future of the Helena May was being discussed in the Council. A question was asked as to whether it still served a useful purpose, as it seemed that there were only 20 residents, there was a decrease in Membership, and a difficulty recruiting Council members. The finances could not stand up to the monthly deficit. Winding up the affairs of the Institute would have to be done by a special Ordinance through the Legislative Council. Marjorie Bray, Mrs A. D. Moore and the Helena May's legal representative, Mr Nigel, met with the Assistant Colonial Secretary, Mr Kidd, on 16 April. The issue of letting the Annexe for a social welfare or charitable object was considered and it was mentioned that the Association for Mentally Handicapped Children and Young People, and the Chinese YWCA were possibly interested.

This was a year designated by the United Nations for focusing on human rights. The China Mail on 15 June had an article by Vincent Shepherd on this theme in which he points out that a Filipino lady had been refused a place in the Helena May, and that this seemed to be racism. He says the enquirer was told by Mrs Millar 'the warden' that 'residential places were restricted to working European women under sixty'. Following publication the Council at its meeting on the 19th decided to ignore the article on the grounds that the writer 'was obviously not in possession of the facts.' Correspondence about the accusation of racism continued in the newspaper with two letters published applauding the writer and berating the Government for taking no action. Miss Eileen Wade, a resident at the Helena May for over 12 years, also took the opportunity to complain about not being allowed to take extra rugs into her room from the vacated Annexe. Mr Shepherd had another article on the same theme published on 14 September, but the Council persisted in its 'no comment' policy.

Despite all these difficulties the Helena May continued to function and an area was cleared and a concrete step made at a cost of $100 so that Mrs Millar could park her car. In August the gardener, who had been receiving $375 per month, had to be given notice. Lee Wing Kee, the family florist business that at one time had a large garden on the site below the Institute and now just has a small hut run by Mr Li and his wife, undertook to look after the grounds for $200 per month. Work started on Kapok Drive behind the Helena May and the construction made it impossible to utilise the rooms for any purpose unless double glazing and reverse cycle air conditioners could be installed.[23]

Fortunately there was soon some good publicity as on 8 November Miss Ng Mei Ling, a world travelling buyer for a department store moved in. There was a photograph and article in the newspaper on 24 December in which the Helena May Secretary, Mrs M. C. Miller, stated: 'We have never done anything to attract Chinese. The food, TV programmes and newspapers provided are all for Europeans and the fact that it costs girls $600 a month to stay has probably kept non-Europeans away.' It was also pointed out that the YWCA provided a parallel service for Chinese girls.

In January 1969 the Council agreed to grant Joan Campbell 'exclusive rights' for ballet classes. In the same month it was noted that the Union Jack was not hoisted on Sundays as the 'boy' had to go through one of the bedrooms and the occupant sometimes slept late. The piano had been refurbished by February and should be 'alright for 5 years'. There was a proposal to change the TV room into a Games Room and buy a table tennis table. The larger of the two side lounges could then become the TV Room.

The City District Officer (CDO) was going to visit the Helena May to discuss the case of Miss Addiscott, who had been asked to find alternative accommodation since she was well over the age allowed for residents and quite probably also earning more than the $2,000 limit per month. It was noted that Caritas also had a 60 year age limit and the YWCA would not accept the birds Miss Addiscott kept. She had approached Mr Anthony Royle MP who in turn had approached the CDO.

Mrs Stafford, who was admitted originally as a transient, had decided that she would like to find a job and stay at the Helena May indefinitely while her husband was a prisoner-of-war in Vietnam. However, as she received a US Government pension of US$600-per month, this plus whatever salary she would earn in a new job would place her above the maximum limit which meant she would have to leave. A petition was received from the Residents asking Council to make an exception in her case, but Council refused. Mrs Hughes, a journalist wished to stay at the Helena May for two to three months at transient rates. She would be charged $30 a day. Transients were required, on two weeks notice, to give up their rooms if they were needed by a 'working girl of the Colony'.

The Helena May unfortunately featured in a negative way in several articles in the *China Mail* and *South China Morning Post* in February and March 1969 because of the dismissal of $305-a-month houseboy So Hoi after 22 years service, and the Institute is described as 'exclusive' because of the room rate. Residents had written a letter of protest to the Council, but Mrs A. D. Moore, the Chairman, commented that they did not have the full facts. Eileen Wade, a former resident and member of the Council who had left the Helena May a year earlier, again was prominent and called a public meeting as she regarded the case 'worse than murder' and called into question labour laws in Hong Kong. Rosemary Inglis writes 'I was a close friend of Phil Salmon, who worked with the library regularly and voluntarily, and I remember she also thought he had been dealt with harshly... the committee never enlightened the people whom he served and as no-one knew who had complained about him and few had a bad word to say against him, there must have been some spitefulness or perhaps something other than his service record involved.'[24] It was noted by the Council that Mr So had been given 'several thousands of dollars from the Chinese staff service fund.' Eileen Wade died some time ago.

In March it was agreed to paint the dining room dark green with white pillars. Also it was noted that the Helena May paid Mrs Millar's return airfare every two years. Francis Johnston, grandson of Lady May, his wife, Paddy, and two children, Helen (12) and James (6), visited the Helena May on 15 April and went on a tour of the premises. An application came from the Prison Department in May for accommodation in the Annexe, but as the prison wardens concerned were male it had to be turned down. By July it was decided that only two amahs would be living on the premises instead of five.

Retiring after Fifty Years

There was a very special event on 30 September when a retirement party was held for two long-serving staff members. Mr Ho Yum Chuen, the "Number One Boy" had served the Helena May for nearly 50 years and was presented with a portable television, which cost $510, with a silver plaque on the side, which cost another $50. Mr Tsang had joined in 1949 and was the "Number One Lounge Boy". He was given a gold watch costing $259.

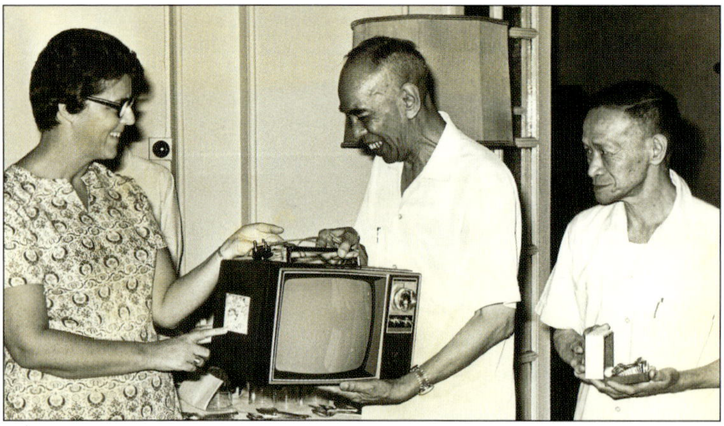

The special condition attached to the Ground Lease from Crown Lands did not permit building for purposes other than the sole use of the Helena May. Thus profit-making projects such as offices, car parks and cinemas had always been refused to other similar organisations. However, the Government was willing to allow the Helena May to sub-let the Annexe to a non-profit-making organization, and there were expressions of interest from various organizations. At the AGM it was agreed that the Scout Association could rent the building, which had been empty for 10 months, because they would not make any real structural alterations, and would occupy it during office hours only. A three-year lease was signed on 23 December.

Sir Murray Maclehose was appointed the 25th Governor of Hong Kong in 1971, and the population was now up to around four million. The April Council Minutes of that year highlight a matter of great concern – it had been noticed that the owner of the flower shop was moving his plants onto the terrace along the side of the Annexe and enquiries with Mr Shin of the Scout Association revealed that he had given permission. There was anxiety about encroachment on the parking area and there had been repeated requests to move the plants. It was pointed out to Mr Shin that the lease to the Scout Association covered the Annexe building only and he had no authority relating to the outside area. The Council agreed that 'the Flower Man must be told he will be charged for use of the land if he continues to use it for flower pots'.

Disaster and opinions in the 70s

The ladies had a great deal more to think about when Typhoon Rose struck on 16 August, making over 5,000 people homeless. The morning after, the damage sustained by the Helena May was assessed. It was mainly the flooding of the whole of the Dining Room in the basement, and flooding of all the rooms on the second floor when the drains became blocked on the roof and

Retirement presentation

the balconies. Residents had to move some of the furniture into the corridor, rugs were taken up, and towels from the linen room were used in mopping-up operations. The strip flooring on the Garden Road side fared better than the parquet floors on the Cotton Tree Drive side. Absolutely nothing could be done about the Dining Room and later the floors had to be re-laid.

In November, due to there being a new Governor and Financial Secretary, it was decided to raise again the possibility of Government agreeing to the re-development of the Helena May Institute site. It was thought that there could be a building with tourist shops on the ground-floor level, which would extend the Peak Tram area, and self-contained bachelor-girl flats on the upper seven or eight floors.

However, two members felt it would be a shame to pull down one of the few remaining old buildings in the Colony. Another suggestion was to move the Institute to another site outside the Central District. This was also opposed as it was thought that the present position, within walking distance of Central, was one of the Helena May's main advantages as it avoided the Residents' need to use transport. One member put forward the idea that, in redeveloping the site, it would be better to build offices rather than shops on the ground floor. Suggestions were then put forward regarding the redevelopment of the Annexe and surrounding area, remembering that in its present state, no profit could be obtained from leasing out the existing building. It could be pulled down and in its place build an indoor swimming pool, bowling alley, squash courts, badminton court and multi-storey car park; and the garden be turned back into tennis courts. It was decided to ask Mr Akers-Jones to find out from Government under what conditions they would allow such redevelopment, and the Legislative Council would be asked if the name could be changed to 'The Helena May Residential Club'.

Several major events occurred in 1972. In June came the worst rainstorm for 83 years in Hong Kong, and it killed over 200 people, mainly in Sau Mau Ping and Kotewall Road, Mid-Levels. The Seawise University ship (the former Queen Elizabeth I) sank in the Rambler Channel after being set on fire, and the Cross-harbour Tunnel was opened. An article appeared on the Rory Kwan page of the *China Mail* on 4 July and is described in the Council Minutes as referring to the Helena May 'in the most derogatory terms':

The Virgins' Retreat doesn't sound a very promising haunt for a naval man who's just stepped off his ship after a few weeks at sea. But according to a little bird, the refined hostel for women which has earned this nickname for obvious reasons, in fact runs the most sophisticated call-girl system in the town. When the American fleet comes in and the officers throw a party, a carefully worded letter goes across to the warden of the hostel asking her to supply so many girls for the occasion. And apparently the men are seldom disappointed.

A strong protest was lodged through solicitors demanding a public apology and the China Mail was to be sued for defamation of character and libel. The residents were advised of this action and told of their right to take action on their own account if they wished. A Mr Summers of The Star contacted the Helena May for an opinion of 'this distasteful article" but the answer was 'No Comment'.

Towards the end of the year it became apparent that due to changing conditions the Annexe could once again be utilised for its original purpose and the Scout Association was informed that their lease would not be renewed.[25] The Council also noted that:

As it was becoming increasingly difficult to find satisfactory house staff, it was decided to eliminate the need for this and, at the same time, to provide the type of accommodation for which there was an increasing demand, by redeveloping the building into twelve self-contained fully furnished flats on the three upper floors each consisting of a bed-sitting room, bathroom and kitchenette with reception office, laundry and storage rooms on the ground floor.

It was decided to amend the Bye-Laws of 1959 so that 'Subscriber Members and their friends may have dinner not more than four times per month in the Dining Room provided they give notice to the Manageress or Steward before 10 a.m. on the day the meal is required.' At a dinner dance, which cost $35, Joan Campbell remembers Ray Cordeiro ('Uncle Ray' who currently can still be heard on local radio) and his band playing

THE COURT OPENS

Work on the Annexe was completed in October and the building was formally opened as The Helena May Court by the Patron, Lady Maclehose on 15 November 1973. It was felt that this facility would further fulfil the aims of The Helena May as there continued to be a steady demand for hostel-type accommodation, and efforts would be made to 'maintain the high standard of comfort and service for which The Helena May has always been known.'[26]

In December it was noted that the car park was in need of resurfacing, and Council members were reminded that it was Government property and $10 a year rent was paid for it. 'There might also be problems with the police as access on to Garden Road was dangerous'. At the January 1974 Council meeting it was recorded that they were not allowed to do anything with the car park land except for the purpose of maintaining the existing buildings, and that it must be handed back in the condition in which it was received.

It was in November of this eventful year - in which the Independent Commission against Corruption was set up, the Terracotta Warriors were discovered in Xian and the Watergate scandal in the US caused Nixon to resign as President – that some members of the Council attended a Legislative Council meeting at which a Private Member's Bill concerning the new constitution was introduced by Mr Bremridge. The Bill was passed on 11 December and the name changed to 'The Helena May'. The word 'Institute' had been dropped because it was felt to be 'outmoded and misleading.'[27] Meanwhile, estimates were obtained for re-roofing the Main Building. Work commenced on 4 December and was completed on the 23rd. The roof was used as a drying area, so while the work was being carried out the drying lines were put in the yard of the Helena May Court.

Copies of the new Constitution were circulated to all Subscriber members and residents in April 1975. In May it was recorded that two double rooms and six single rooms were empty, and in the following month another double room was also empty. It was suggested that the Helena May should stop serving food. However, by October the situation was looking better with only one double room and three single rooms vacant. It was noted that the resident in Room 25 was a Filipina maid. Her employer was living in the Mandarin Hotel and was not paying the bills.

ENDNOTES

1 Mellor, 1980, Vol I, p.107
2 Update of History in 1950 – p.17
3 Gittens, 1969, p. 189-198
4 Update of History in 1950 – p.18
5 Update of History in 1950 – p.19
6 *South China Morning Post* 17 February 1947
7 Update of History in 1950 – p.20
8 Transcript of interview with Dorothy Collins by Gill Townsend October 2000
9 Hazzard, 200, p.69 and p.79
10 Personal communication via Rosemary Inglis to Esther Morris July 2006
11 Gittens, 1969, p.219
12 Interview with Rosemary Inglis by Jenny Day and Esther Morris July 2006
13 Personal communication to Esther Morris July 2006
14 Update of History in 1963 – p.21
15 Interview with Joan Campbell by Jenny Day, Feb 2005
16 Personal communication via Rosemary Inglis to Esther Morris July 2006
17 A story from an ex-resident – *The Helena May Newsletter* April 2004
18 Personal communication to Esther Morris, March 2006
19 Transcript of interview with Dorothy Collins by Gill Townsend October 2000
20 Update of History in 1969 – p.23
21 A story from an ex-resident – *The Helena May Newsletter* April 2004
22 Council Minutes October 1967
23 Update of History in 1969 – p.23
24 Personal communication to Esther Morris July 2006
25 Update of History in January 1974 – p.25
26 Update of History in January 1974 – p.26
27 Update of History in November 1979 – p.27

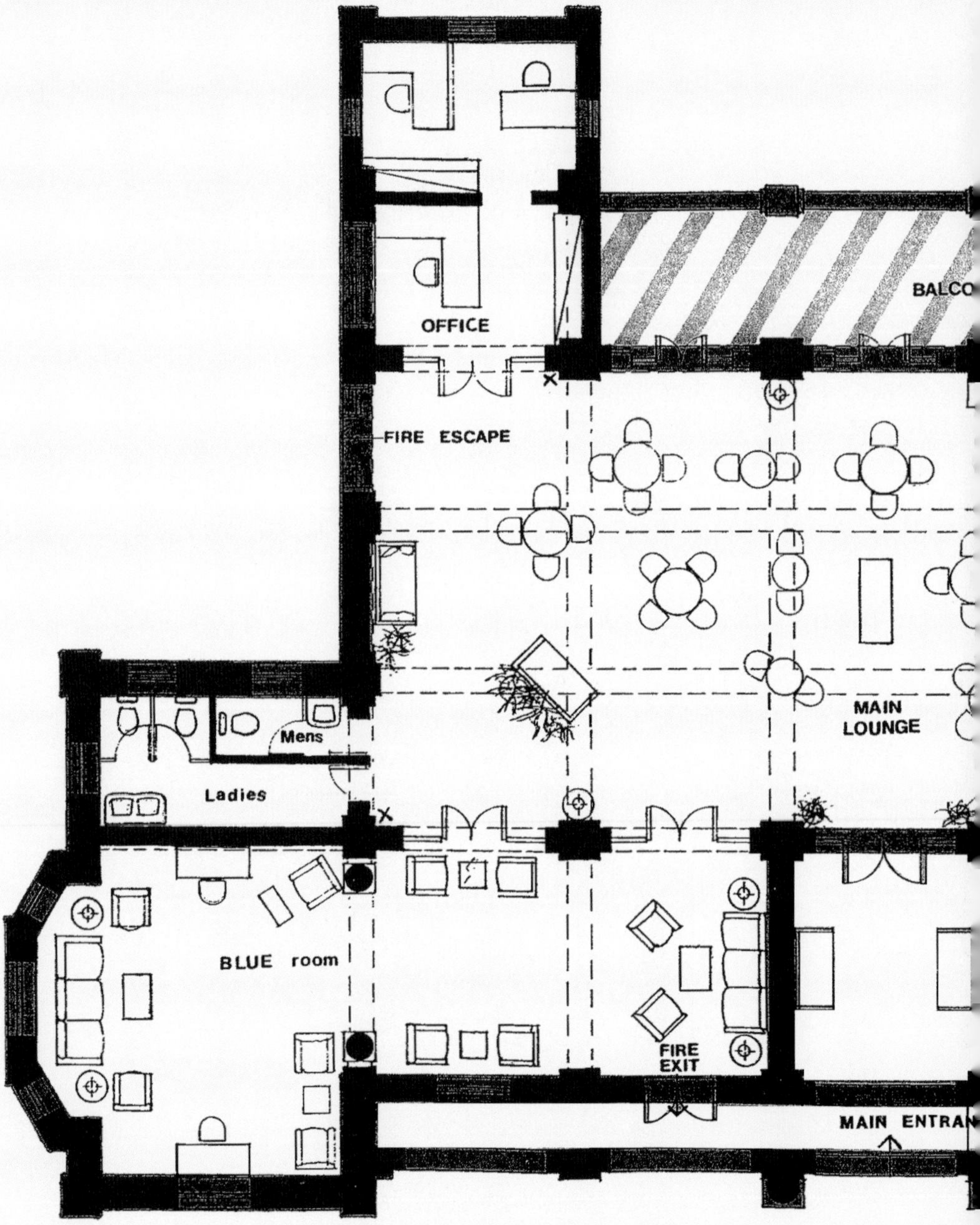
OFFICE
BALCO
FIRE ESCAPE
Mens
Ladies
MAIN
LOUNGE
BLUE room
FIRE
EXIT
MAIN ENTRAN

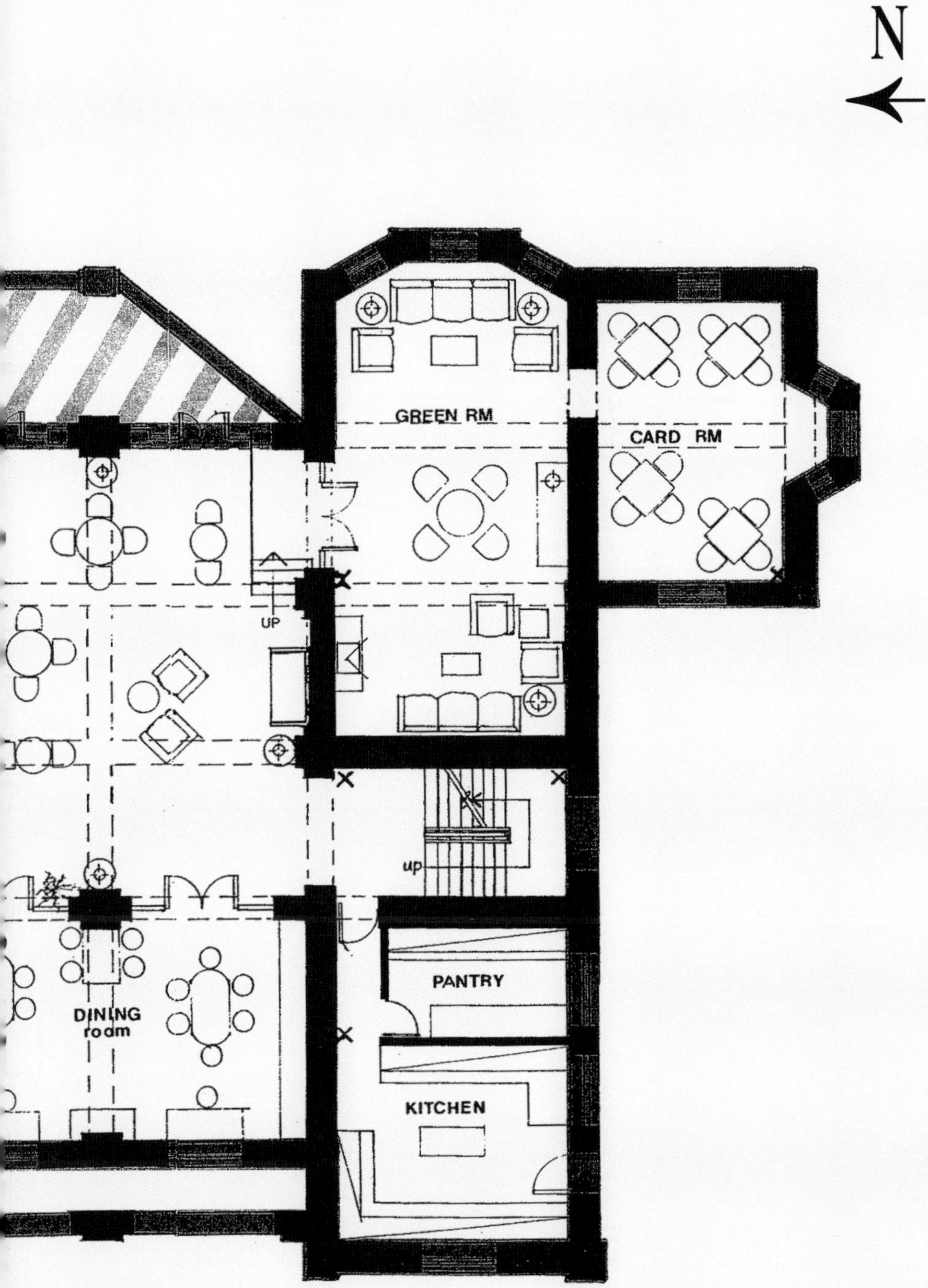

Plan of the ground floor after the library moved downstairs

CODA PLAZA

5. *The Last 30 Years: 1977 to 2006*

The Vietnam War had now ended, Chiang Kai Shek had died, the Cultural Revolution had ended and Mao Tse-tung had died. At the Helena May costs were ever increasing for both maintenance and overheads – necessitating small increases in the residential rates, though every effort was made to keep these to a minimum whilst maintaining the high standards. Mrs Parker, who had been Manageress for many years, left in March 1977. This was the year Ocean Park opened, and at the Helena May major works in modernisation, re-wiring, and re-decoration were carried out in the main building 'thus enhancing the existing facilities and pleasant atmosphere which have always been a feature of the success of the Helena May.'[1]

This was also the time when Winsome Lane came to Hong Kong and stayed at the Helena May until 1992.[2] She had been in Jamaica as a Reuter's correspondent and wrote to the *South China Morning Post* as she had heard about Hong Kong from contacts that had been there. She was employed by them as a columnist but realized that she couldn't afford other accommodation. When her daughters visited her from UK they found it hilarious that their mother was staying in a sort of boarding school with rules and regulations. She remembered that the rule in the Court was no visitors after midnight and none at all Monday to Friday. She reminisced about a local personality courting a very sexy girl who stayed in the Court, and one night he broke down her door. One positive aspect of staying at the Helena May was the lack of thefts, but on the negative side there was a shortage of laundry facilities. She remembered the traditional Christmas dinner for Residents when guests could be invited. When she arrived, the rent was $1000 per month, plus $15 for dinner; when she moved out 15 years later the rent for a corner room was $15,000.

In the year that Margaret Thatcher became Prime Minister in Britain, 1979, "Prefontaine" wine was made available in the Lounge from 19 December – though, according to Council Minutes, very few glasses were being ordered. In June 1980, Mr Sinn of the contractors Sinn & Company presented the Helena May with a large mounted photograph of the building taken immediately after completion of recent redecoration of the outside. Gail Buttifant was appointed afternoon librarian on 1 July, and later in the year Marjorie Bray joined the Council. These two ladies have been mainstays of the Helena May and played major roles in the continuance of its traditions, while at the same time supporting future changes. One tradition that was being questioned in December was the smoking policy as there had been requests for a no smoking area, preferably in the Blue Room. It was decided that the bay window end could be non-smoking.

In the same month the Antiquities Advisory Board sent some representatives to the Helena May in connection with the preservation of old buildings. The three visitors were Dr Solomon Bard (a well-known figure in Hong Kong), an architect and a photographer. The report on the Board's meeting in February 1981[3] notes:

6. Historically, the importance of The Helena May must not be judged in the light of great events, but in the impact on the day-to-day life of ordinary people. So viewed it filled an important need and played its part in making Hong Kong what it is – a successful and thriving place. More than merely providing an accommodation, badly needed, it also contributed a good deal to the cultural life of Hong Kong by providing a place for concerts, lectures, and various classes, as well as a good library.

10. The present 75-year lease, which has many restrictions, expires in 1983. The Council of The Helena May has apparently no plans for re-development. The building stands in a prominent place on Garden Road and is a well-known landmark of early Hong Kong. Its architecture and historical merits make it an item worthy of consideration for preservation as a monument.

The census of this year counted the population to be around five million. In April a property survey was carried out by the company Vigers because of concern about the redevelopment of St John's Building on the plot below the Helena May on Garden Road. The survey showed the structure to be sound, with just minor defects due to normal wear and tear. However, there was a termite infestation in the lower area.

Renowned yoga teacher Thelma Heitmeyer restarted her class in July and the hall was also hired by the Weight Watchers group. At the Council meeting on 8 October it was noted that paintings by Helena's sister had been donated and were to be framed and hung in the lounge.

The florist at Lee Wing Kee was asked again to remove his plants from the car park area in August 1982, and Thelma Heitmeyer's yoga class was attended by Lady Muriel Kadoorie, wife of Lord Lawrence, who was nephew of Sir Ellis. A young Esther Morris, who became member number 4436 on 8 November, was also in the class. The new Library was opened downstairs in part of the former Ballroom on 17 November with a plaque laid by Lady Youde, wife of the new Governor, Sir Edward Youde. The smaller room of the old library was to be the Residents' sitting room.

The wrangle with the "Flower Man" continued into 1983, when he was advised by the solicitors that he could be charged HK$80 – 100 per square metre per annum. He continued to ignore the situation. No-one could ignore the damage caused by Typhoon Ellen in September. However, everything was

Mr Sinn's photo of Helena May

cleared up in time for the visit of Helena May's grand-daughter, Margaret Osmaston, from 26 to 28 October. Marjorie Bray, with whom she had been at school, organised a luncheon in her honour, which was attended by Lady Youde and Lady Haddon-Cave.

SEVENTY YEARS OLD

On 1 September 1984 Shirley Eltringham became resident manageress. Robyn McLean of the Public Records Office started compiling a new short history of the Helena May in February 1985, and Winsome Lane had an article about the place published in *The Lady* on 23 October 1986. She writes:

Entering the Helena May's cavernous lounge from the heat of the street is like visiting another world, a world of colonial leisure and easy living long past in Hong Kong. The cool public rooms offer a comfortable retreat from the concrete jungle and stressful life of the modern city... here the residents live a life of old-world comfort and style – at a cost far below any other acceptable living accommodation in Hong Kong today. There is always a long waiting list... Cab-drivers all know it and will often bring girls here if they arrive, as many youngsters still do, with no arranged place to stay... Chinese and expatriate applicants for accommodation are treated exactly the same and there is always a high proportion of Chinese residents, although no Chinese food is served... Membership is open to men and a High Court judge or high ranking civil servant can often be seen about. There are now about 40 residents in the two buildings. Membership of the club is over one thousand. The lease will expire in three years. A renewal has been applied for, but the outcome is uncertain since Hong Kong will revert to Chinese government in 1997, and the fate of this pleasant and useful building is yet to be revealed. If the lease is not renewed, the land could sell for enormous sums to one of the property developers. If it goes, an institution in the cross-cultural life of Hong Kong will have been lost and the city will be the poorer.

One aspect of the Helena May that has been a constant theme relates to culture. Throughout the years members have been able to enjoy drama, concerts, talks, study groups, art exhibitions, and tours around various places in Hong Kong. One such event was held in April 1987 when a group of ladies explored Chinese monuments in the New Territories with the multi-talented Dr Solomon Bard.

From September of that year until May 1989 the ballet school premises on the lower ground floor were rented out in the mornings to the Specialist Academy, which was run by Anthea Strickland. This later became the Winchester International School when it moved to its permanent premises in Sai Wan Ho.

A Helena May trip to the New Territories with Dr Solomon Bard
Rosemary Lee is on the far right

Tiananmen Square and Future Uncertainty

Hong Kong and China's history will forever be marked by the events in Tiananmen Square, Beijing, on 4 June 1989. The student protests, the deaths and the subsequent demonstrations have had ongoing repercussions. The Chinese population of Hong Kong became increasingly nervous of the future reunification with China and some people made plans to obtain passports elsewhere for themselves, or at least for their children, as a form of insurance. The Helena May, it seems, just carried on with business as usual.

The appointment of Vijai Singh as Manager in March 1991 brought about some changes.[4] She felt that the Helena May needed to be more inviting and progressive and she had the entire premises repainted and then began hiring out rooms for public functions such as weddings, cocktail parties and fashion shows. In those days only one function could take place at a time. The first big fashion show was with Agnes B, but Vijai particularly enjoyed the weddings and christenings. Hong Kong's population was still growing and in the census of this year was calculated to be 5.86 million.

The residents during the 90s were secretaries with law firms and investment companies, and supply teachers. They all tended to be very glamorous. There was an elected resident's representative, who would notify the management of problems by leaving a note at the office before 9.00am. The residents would come to Vijai Singh, who was a trained nurse, with problems relating to their health, their work, and adjusting to life in Hong Kong. Vijai held very strongly to the rule of no male guests in the bedrooms and has many amusing memories of foiling attempts to cross the line, particularly men seen sneaking up the stairs thinking she wasn't watching! Those years also saw an increase in the number of Chinese members. She made a point of greeting people as she passed through the premises and recalled that she was always willing to join in when a project required an extra pair of hands.

A committee of five residents helped to organize the annual March balls. The first one, in 1992, had a polka dot theme with big clusters of polka dot balloons around the ballroom. In 1993 the theme was pink and most attendees entered into the spirit of the event sporting appropriately coloured dresses, blouses, camisoles, feather boas, scarves, flowers, jackets, waistcoats and ties.

An important event occurred in this year. Following the earlier interest of the Antiquities Advisory Board in the Helena May, on 8 October the exterior façade of the main building became a Declared Monument under the Antiquities and Monuments Ordinance. However, with the approach of the end of colonial rule, a period of uncertainty was likely. No one could guess at this time, with 700 subscriber members, just how uncertain the future would be. Towards the end of the year the Council again considered redevelopment.

This fitted in with Council's vision to see the Helena May through the handover and into the 21st century as a viable Club moving with the times, meeting the demands of modern life in Hong Kong whilst maintaining our traditions and remits under our Ordinance.[5]

A short ceremony was held on 24 January 1994 to mark the Gazetting of the exterior as a historical building. During the rest of that year the Helena May set out to comply with the stringent standards of the Club Ordinance and the Licensing Authority (Safety of Premises Act). The Government required several alterations to be made. This was a very costly exercise (over $3m) and it was agreed that the work could be spread over several years. Vijai Singh's main project, besides organising the multi-coloured ball in March, was to refurbish the fire services and rewire the entire premises. She managed to get the requirement of a sprinkler system waived as it would have been far too expensive at the time.

Over the next ten years the Helena May undertook a long list of work, the scale and cost of which was beyond anything previously faced. Implementing these requirements depleted the reserves and strained the resources of the organisation, which had no endowment and no benefactor to step in and help out. It was the duty of the Council to seriously consider all options for survival. Many fund-raising activities were launched, along with increases in fees and subscriptions. In October 1995 members received a letter from the Chairman regarding the Helena May's obligations and responsibilities to women as set out in its Constitution. The Council had concluded that it was 'worthwhile investigating the feasibility of a re-development of the area presently occupied by the Court... the re-development would be separate from the Main Building (its outside already deemed an historic site for preservation) but a section would be allocated for exclusive use by the Helena May'. Accommodation would be lost but all hoped the scheme could generate sufficient funds to assure a better future and facilities.

An application was submitted to the Town Planning Board in April 1996 to redevelop the Court into a 22 storey serviced apartment building. It was rejected 'primarily on the grounds that the nature of the proposed development was predominantly non-institutional and did not comply with the planning intention for the site.'[6] Although the decision went for review on 8 November, it was still not approved. Meanwhile, as a fundraiser a Gala Dinner was held at Government House to coincide with the 80th anniversary of the Helena May.

Bearing in mind that Hong Kong was to become a Special Administrative Region of China on 1 July 1997, the ball's theme for that year was 'East meets West' with decorations of Chinese crackers and lanterns. As usual naval men were among the guests and the proceeds from the ball were used to purchase necessities for the residents. The Helena May also hosted Murder Mysteries and plays, but Vijai Singh remembers the humidity sometimes played havoc with the staging of these events.

Membership numbers had started to decline as expatriates had been leaving Hong Kong in the years leading up to the 'hand over'. The Helena May farewelled its Patron, the last Governor's wife Lavender Patten, and welcomed Betty Tung, the wife of the new Chief Executive, Tung Chee Hwa. An economic crisis in Asia occurred just as Hong Kong relinquished its British sovereignty and severely challenged the already strapped finances of the Helena May. This plus the introduction of work permits in April of this memorable year resulted in a most precarious situation. The Council had to look at alternative ways forward. 'Key questions began to arise as to whether we needed planning permission on the site, the size of the building in relation to the building and non-building land and also various nuances of interpreting our lease conditions.'[7] The *Proposed Redevelopment* document explained the situation:

With the help of development consultants Larry Tam and Associates in July 1997 we invited initial expressions of interest from 25 developers to enter into a joint venture with the Helena May to partially redevelop the site without the need for planning permission. This means that the developer should be responsible at his own expense to demolish the existing HM Court and construct a new hostel building on the same site. The developer would also be required to fund the refurbishment of the existing HM Main Building. It is proposed that the developer shall be appointed to manage, maintain and operate the new hostel building for a fixed term of years (probably around 20), and share the revenue with the HM on a basis to be agreed. The developer shall also make a lump sum payment to the HM upon signing of a joint venture agreement.

...Three expressions of interest were received thus confirming interest in the project and its potential viability. Tender documentation is currently being drawn up and all the initial developers approached will be formally requested to submit their detailed proposals by sealed tender. It is intended that this should happen when the economic climate has improved.

...In order to provide guidance to any developer, our requirements for the refurbishment of the Main Building need to be determined in order to estimate the costs for tender purposes... we appointed Leigh and Orange Architects who have helped with this process. These ideas are closely linked to our membership requirements, the future management of the club and how we see ourselves developing as a club.

In order to know what to do, we need to have a clear vision of our club's future and understand our members' needs and desires. We are currently investigating whether to take on the Peninsula Clubs Group to advise us about future management of the Club. ...Our current Constitution controls our membership categories. It may be necessary to change our Constitution, when we have decided where we are going. We have been investigating various options available to us.[8]

In December Helena's granddaughter Margaret Osmaston visited again, along with her daughter, Liz Hampshire and four grandchildren. They were en route

__1__-Allen Youngblood at the piano. __2__-Roy Spencer, Esther Morris, John Dodwell & Mrs Spencer 1986. __3__-Dorothy Collins & Lavender Patten 1996. __4__-Lord & Lady Kadoorie. __5__-Rosanna Yue's retirement in 1998. __6__-Anna Wu, Teresa Norton, Anson Chan & Council members 2001. __7__-Selina Tsang & Marjory Bent 2006. __8__-Joan Campbell & Marjorie Bray 2005. __9__-Lorette Roberts & Betty Tung. __10__-Shirley Hazzard 2005. __11__-An evening of Shakespeare with Daniel Foley 2006.

to Australia and had tea at the Helena May with Marjorie Bray. By February 1998 Marjorie had been persuaded to become Council Chairman, at a time when the place was operating with half its usual number of residents and the membership had fallen from nearly 700 to just above 400. Rosanna Yue retired as Treasurer in May after 30 years of service. A few months into her Chairmanship, Marjorie invited Letty Chiu Chabot to become the first Chinese Council member for 50 years:

...as she (Marjorie) was well aware that the future of the club had to include a greater number of the local community. She tried very hard to recruit new members and to invite other Chinese members to the Council. In order to give the Helena May a higher profile she gave interviews to the press and on the radio, and generously used her extensive personal network to obtain support for the Club.[9]

One such effort was a talk to the Hong Kong Women's Corona Society on 14 September, at which Marjorie gave a picture of Hong Kong as it was when the Helena May Institute for Women was founded, and outlined the current situation. She ended:

Meanwhile we have a gracious building, which would lend itself to music. Helena May was a hospitable, loving and very musical lady and we could fill the place with music in her memory. I hope we can make full use of the building as well as give a service to Hong Kong.

In 1999 a move to open up accommodation in the Court to couples and men served to ameliorate the situation somewhat, though the Helena May still did not feel very secure. There were many changes at Council level, but it was determined to continue with the idea to re-develop the Court believing the project to be the only way to guarantee the organization's viability. At an Extraordinary General Meeting held on 21 January a resolution was passed to proceed with the planned re-development. Architects, planners, consultants, lawyers and accountants who had volunteered their services attended the meeting. However, with a deepening economic recession, no developers came forward willing to participate in the joint venture. Problems were compounded by government disinterest, repeated rejections by the Town Planning Board and objections raised by the Traffic and the Lands Departments. The Helena May faced the daunting predicament of merely existing.

But by April it had its first Chinese general manager – Yolanda Wong. Within six months the first floor of the Main Building was fully occupied, after having been closed for more than a year, and the Court was full. At this time hours of operation were extended to 9.30pm. Over the next few years Yolanda oversaw the hiring of new staff members and also helped the Council to renovate the entire main Building and garden area and redevelop the Court Building.[10]

Annelise Connell, having been away from Hong Kong for almost 30 years, returned and lived in the Main Building for 8 months from 1999-2000. During this time she heard many stories from 'girls' who were visiting Hong Kong and staying at 'the May' where they had been residents many years ago.

2000 Brings New Vigour

The year 2000 came and the Helena May saw new vigour from the Council, newly appointed staff, and a new determination to re-invent itself. New ideas, new events, new liaisons with groups like the Friends of the Art Museum of Chinese University, plus diversity in membership, all served to upgrade the image and build confidence. The new century also saw the bursting of the "dot.com" bubble and the collapse of the technology stock bonanza. This exacerbated the gloomy economic picture and further reductions in operating costs at the Helena May were no longer possible, the only way was to take a deep breath and go forward. It was imperative that revenue be generated from catering, accommodation, hire of hall activities, events and subscriptions. Many brave steps were taken such as providing an improved dinner service and, importantly, installing air-conditioners in the Main Lounge and Dining Room.

'March Art' in 2001 presented a wonderful opportunity to showcase the special qualities of the Helena May. This was a festival of art, music, literature and cuisine, a week-long tribute to women in the arts with all profits going to charities Harmony House and Growing Together. Also a non-smoking policy was introduced and a Conference Centre was opened in what had been storage and laundry rooms in the basement. The English Speaking Union was accommodated in the Helena May from summer 2001 – housing their library and holding activities there – until summer 2004, when they moved to permanent premises. A party to celebrate the 85th anniversary featured the Welsh Male Voice Choir in a freshly painted, gracefully decorated Main Room of which members could feel justifiably proud.

The Council chose to disband the Re-development Committee in 2002 after further obstructions by government departments and no positive response from any developer. This critical decision, made with the consultants involved, was a prudent and wise step. Clearly, the Helena May would have to rely on itself. It was decided instead to invest scarce dollars to raise the accommodation standards and future income potential by completely renovating the interior of the Court flatlets with up-to-date kitchens and bathrooms and re-decorating the bedrooms of the Main Building.

By 2003 the 14 studio apartments were fully occupied and the following year two further studios were added. A new Food & Beverage Committee was formed to raise the standards of the menus, introduce a wine list and generally improve member satisfaction. Allen Youngblood and friends started their monthly Monday evening performances in September of that year, and this brought in more members and guests for dinner. The staff had also undergone many changes, cooks made way for chefs, trained waiters wore smart uniforms and a restaurant manager was employed. As always, the staff responded with loyalty and diligence.

THE SARS CRISIS

These qualities were needed when Hong Kong and the whole of Asia was hit with the SARS crisis. Severe Acute Respiratory Syndrome caught the world by surprise and an epidemic was feared. Hong Kong shut down and it would be three to four months before travel and business resumed. Fortunately, with strict hygiene precautions in place, members were able to find a healthy welcome at the Helena May. Tables were often full at lunchtime with members and guests avoiding public restaurants, and mothers brought their children along when schools were closed. Meanwhile garden plans began to take root; a logo was selected from submissions made by members; a brochure was printed; and greater communication via e-mail and newsletter prompted more member involvement and awareness in the organization's activities, its history and its future.

Public opinion about conservation of historic monuments in Hong Kong began to challenge government inertia. Media focus on the fate of Kom Tong Hall – the home that Ho Kom Tong had built in Mid-Levels in 1914 – occasioned a heightened sensitivity to the need for the Helena May to continue as a valuable part of Hong Kong's heritage. In memory of her grandfather, Dr Stella Ho Pak-Ngor generously donated 1,000 pounds sterling to the history fund. It was with considerable pleasure and pride that the Helena May was able to invite the families of Ho Kom Tong and Sir Ellis Kadoorie to attend events in the main lounge.

One of the Helena May's longest serving members of staff retired in March 2004. Robert To started as a porter in the court in 1976, and later became the odd-job man who did everything from delivering messages to assisting the office staff. Moving with the times was demonstrated when the 'Cyber Corner' was opened in April so that members and residents could catch up on emails or surf the web. The initiatives to make the Helena May 'the best it could be' were well demonstrated at the opening of the re-landscaped garden and patio, and the Garden Room, on 11 September. This was an expensive project but one which would add all round benefit. As with all the organization's undertakings, a committee of dedicated volunteers, led by Letty Chiu Chabot, provided the incentives and energy, along with the ever supportive staff.

However, the most important achievement of that year was the least apparent. The Licensing Authority granted an exemption from the requirement to install a sprinkler system in the ground floor public rooms. Relief was palpable; the onerous tasks commenced in 1994 were finally complete. In the December Newsletter new Chairman of Council Marjory Bent writes:

Under the outstanding management of our departing General Manager, Yolanda Wong, the Helena May has experienced exceptional growth, stability and popularity.

New General Manager, Betty Simpson, started work on 7 December, describing herself as '95 percent Chinese'. Apparently she had an English ancestor in Shanghai and still carries his name. With such a background, and many admirable qualifications and qualities, she is an ideal person to continue the good work in a multicultural institution.

A tea-party was held on 12 January 2005 in traditional Helena May style to say farewell to long-time members Marjorie Bray and her husband Denis, who were leaving Hong Kong. Marjorie was given Honorary Life Membership for all that she had done for the Helena May during her many years as member, Council member and Chairman. Sadly Denis died just a few months later.

Joan Campbell's long association was recognised by her being guest of honour at the International Women's Day tea on 8 March, when she regaled the audience with tales of being a resident and a ballet teacher. Some of her ex-pupils, who have gone on to become successful in the field, joined the event and indicated how special Joan is to them. Having become resident at the Court, Joan demonstrates her faith in the Helena May.

Members were thrilled to be able to welcome novelist Shirley Hazzard at a luncheon event in the Garden Room during the Literary Festival in March. She recounted tales of her own post-Second World War time in Hong Kong and memories of the Helena May – which she was very pleased to see had retained its fundamental character during her 57-year absence.

All three of these ladies fondly remembered the days of wicker settees, chairs and tables in the Lounge, and there was perhaps a hint of regret that life was not quite so 'genteel' as it once had been. However, the transformation of the former Ballroom into the now multi-purpose Garden Room has brought back some of the elegance of earlier eras, and meals can once again be served in the room where residents used to take their breakfast and dinner. This lovely high-ceiling room with elegantly arched windows now has attractive curtains, chandeliers and large mirrors. At night the fairy lights in the trees in the garden are reflected inside. The grand staircase down which the young women could make their entrance has long since gone – but changes are ongoing. Just before leaving Hong Kong in March Chairman of Council (2002-2004) Elizabeth Cote wrote:

A Club full of promise for its future is to be found housed in a historic building known as the Helena May. Serious about its primary position as a place for women, perfectly at ease with its gentlemen members, and growing more confident in its relevance to Hong Kong, The Helena May has definite plans to continue with certainty.

THE HELENA MAY LOOKS TO THE FUTURE

To this end the Council had taken the step of engaging a firm of professional architects/designers to assist the Long-Range Strategic Planning Committee 'to investigate the most appropriate way to plan for the future of the Helena May over the coming five to 10 years, based on thorough research.'[11] As part of the process a major professional survey of members was planned for later in the year.

Gail Buttifant celebrated her 25th anniversary as librarian in July and was warmly praised for her innovations, contributions and dedication. Throughout the years, the Library has continued to be a source of stability and refuge. Many members' children have benefited from the wide range of books available, the story telling sessions, and the introduction to a certain way of life that comes with the joy of becoming engrossed in reading in an appropriate setting. New books continue to be added every month and there are periodic sales of old books. The Library Committee members seem adamant in their defence of the card index system, which is in itself a tangible part of the Helena May's history. While that system may be retained, Gail decided she would retire on 30 June 2006.

Towards the end of the year the Council decided to form a Community Outreach Committee with Marge Lo as Chairman. This group quickly had several projects underway. Some members were helping to teach English in local primary schools, and links were being forged with people working on education projects for impoverished children in China. The Helena May has always helped various charities and non-profit making organizations through fundraising, book donations or providing meeting rooms. The Royal Asiatic Society and the Royal Geographical Society often hold their events at the Helena May, and in recent years the following charities have been helped in different ways:

- *Christian Action*
- *Crossroads International*
- *Growing Together*
- *Harmony House*
- *Hong Kong Arts Festival Student Ticket Scheme*
- *ROSE Charities Cambodia*
- *Society for Community Organization*
- *Springboard Project*
- *The Community Advice Bureau*
- *The Home of Loving Faithfulness*
- *The Hong Kong Breast Cancer Foundation*
- *The Matilda Child Development Centre*
- *The Remar Association*
- *Outlying Island Women's Association*

On 8 December 2005 the Council entertained the Helena May's new patron, Mrs Selina Tsang, wife of Hong Kong's second Chief Executive. Since she moved into Government House in 2006, and so lives virtually next door like our founding patron did, it is hoped she will take advantage of the Helena May's facilities.

Whilst some, noticeably male, newspaper columnists still harp on about the 'regimented boarding school image' and the 'no gentlemen visitors after 10pm' rule, it is encouraging to have the views of someone who has lived in Hong Kong for ten years and at the Court for nearly four years. For Leanne Stoiche, the Helena May is 'a relaxing haven' where she can escape from the rush and stress of the city. She says the staff members are 'wonderful' and have become just like family. Their caring attitude makes all the difference to residents living far away from their own families, and visitors notice the 'nurturing feeling' of the place.[12] In February 2006 there were women from Britain, Australia, America and several European countries as well as Chinese ladies. Their occupations included fashion designer, dance teacher, paralegal, editor, teacher and doctor. Although the rooms are not too spacious, the residents effectively live in a grand mansion house and have the run of the place. 'There is nowhere else quite like it'.

In this 90th anniversary year, with Hong Kong's population at around seven million, the Helena May continues to look after women and children in the spirit of its foundation – it still accommodates single working women, and plays its part in building bridges between cultures by being a centre for community work. No-one knows what challenges the future will bring, but hopefully there will continue to be women in Hong Kong who are willing to give their time to conserve the Helena May for many years to come, and who will be inspired by the work of the pioneering women who have left behind this wonderful legacy.

ENDNOTES

1 Update of History in November 1979 – p.27
2 Interviewed by Jenny Day March 2005
3 An extract from Board Paper AAB/2/81
4 Interviewed by Jenny Day March 2005
5 *Proposed Redevelopment of the Helena May Court* p.1
6 *Proposed Redevelopment of the Helena May Court* p.1
7 *Proposed Redevelopment of the Helena May Court* p.1
8 *Proposed Redevelopment of the Helena May Court* p.2
9 Farewell to Marjorie Bray – speech by Letty Chiu Chabot on 12 January 2005
10 Farewell Yolanda – article by Meredith Cox, *The Helena May Newsletter* December 2004
11 Marjory Bent *The Helena May Newsletter* January-March 2005
12 As told to Jenny Day 22 February 2006

Helena and Henry's family tree

- **Helena Augusta Victoria Barker** (1863-1945)
  married to **Francis Henry May** (1860-1922)
  - **Stella** (1892-1966) | Major General Philip **De Fonblanque** (1885-1940).
    - Anne (1921-1978)
    - **Mary**(1923-) | Hugh **Duncan**
    - Tony (1926-2003)
  - **Phoebe** (1895-1975) | Rev. George Elwes Allen **Whitworth** (1888-1969)
    - **Andrew** (1927-)
    - **Margaret** (1930-) | M. F. **Osmaston**
      - Four children, including daughter **Liz Hampshire**
    - **Timothy** (1932-)
  - **Iris** (1898-1989) | Professor Edward Hamilton **Johnston** (died 1942)
    - **Francis** (1925-) | Patricia (**Paddy**) (died 1995)
      - **Helen** (1958-)
      - **James** (1964-2006)
    - Katharine (1927-)
    - Edward (1929-1991)
    - Felicity (1930-)
    - Stephen (1934-)
    - **Veronica** (1936-)
  - **Dione** (1900-1963) | -**Kinchin Smith** (1895-1958)
    - **Michael** (1921-2002) | **Rachel**
      - Five Children, including son Peter | **Alexandra**
    - **Lorna** (1922-) | Kenneth **Headlam-Morley** (1901-1982)

The names in **bold** indicate those members of the family who are mentioned in the text.

——— Children of

——— Married to

Chronology of Events related to The Helena May

1863	• Helena Barker born on 27 March
1890	• The Barker family arrived in Hong Kong. • The Hong Kong Benevolent Society set up as a ladies' charitable committee • 31 August: Helena married Henry May
1909	• YWCA housed in Beaconsfield Arcade
1912	• 4 July: Henry sworn in as 15th Governor of Hong Kong
1913	• Miss Eyre's YWCA merged with the Hong Kong Benevolent Society
1914	• 22 January: Ellis Kadoorie offered money for the Helena May Institute • 30 January: Ho Kom Tong offered a matching sum • The erection of the Helena May Institute commenced
1916	• 12 September: the Helena May Institute opened • Library wing built • Resident Matron engaged
1919	• Three classrooms on first floor converted into bedrooms
1921	• Basement made into a dining hall and cloakroom
1922	• Resident secretary added to staff
1923	• Tennis court laid
1928	• Part-time librarian appointed
1929	• Office with veranda added for secretary • Old office converted into a members' cloakroom • Old cloakroom converted into a pantry • November: Premises rented in Kowloon • Bronze tablet placed in the entrance hall
1932	• Full-time librarian appointed
1933	• Kowloon branch moved to Boundary Street
1941	• December: Building taken over by Public Works Department • Japanese used the Helena May building to house troops and to stable horses
1944	• Building selected to be used as a public library • 5 December: The library eventually opened
1945	• August: Japan surrendered (VJ Day) • October: Helena died at Clare Hall in Suffolk • RAF took over the building as their headquarters
1946	• December: RAF handed the building back
1947	• The Helena May Institute reopened to members • Tennis net purchased and posts put up • Carol Bateman dancing school started
1953	• The first associate (male) member joined
1954	• Extension to library built with servants' quarters below
1956	• Building began of the Annexe to accommodate 16 residents
1957	• 10 July: cornerstone for the Annexe, built on part of the tennis court, laid by Lady Grantham
1958	• 13 March: Annexe opened by Lady Black
1961	• Air conditioning installed in the Library
1963	• Bachelors granted associate membership
1966	• Work on Kapok (now Cotton Tree) Drive was started
1967	• August: riots by communists; several residents left
1968	• 1 January: Annexe closed • Carol Bateman left
1969	• 23 December: lease with the Scouts' Association signed
1973	• Annexe reopened as Court with 12 self-contained studio flats
1974	• Name changed from the 'The Helena May Institute' to 'The Helena May'
1982	• October: Library moved downstairs into part of the former Ballroom
1988	• September: The Specialist Academy opened in the ballet school premises
1993	• 8 October: the exterior of the main building became a declared monument
1996	• 80th anniversary of the opening – Gala dinner at Government House
2002	• Competition to design a logo
2003	• December: Helena May Newsletter started
2004	• Garden re-opened; Garden Room opened
2006	• 12 September: 90th anniversary of the opening

Bibliography

Administrative Report, 1913, 1916 Hong Kong Government Reports Online (1853-1941)

Airlie, Shona (1989) *Thistle and Bamboo: the life and times of Sir James Stewart Lockhart*, Hong Kong: Oxford University Press

Angus, Marjorie Bird (1985) *Bamboo Connection*, Hong Kong: Heinemann

Barker, Kathleen E. (1996) *Change and Continuity: a history of St Stephen's Girls' College, Hong Kong 1906-1996*, Hong Kong: St Stephen's Girls' College

Benson, Stella (1931) 'On Using a Library' in *St John's Review*, Vol. II, p.7

Benson, Stella (published 1978) *Some letters of Stella Benson, 1928-1933*, edited by Cecil Clarabut, Hong Kong: Libra Press

Bloomfield, F. (1984) *Hong Kong's Street Names and Their Origins, Vol.1* Hong Kong: Urban Council

Brownfoot, Janice, N. (1984) 'Memsahib in Malaya', in Callan, Hilary & Ardener, Shirley (eds) *The Incorporated Wife* London: Croom Helm

Buruma, I. (1989) 'Introduction', in Davis, B. (ed) *Historic Postcards of Hong Kong: from the private collection of Arthur Hacker*. Hong Kong: Stock House Productions

Blue Book for the Year 1912, Hong Kong: Hong Kong Government

Blue Book for the year 1916, Hong Kong: Hong Kong Government

Colonial Report (1918), Colonial Secretary M. Fletcher, Hong Kong: Hong Kong Government

Cooper, Suzanne Fagence (2001) *The Victorian Woman*, London: V & A Publications

Courtauld, Caroline (1997) *The Hong Kong Story*, Hong Kong: Oxford University Press

Crisswell, C. & Watson, M. (1982) *The Royal Hong Kong Police, 1841-1945*, Hong Kong: Macmillan

Elegant, R.S. (1977) *Dynasty*, London: Collins

Endacott, G.B. (1964) *A History of Hong Kong* (Second Edition) Hong Kong: Oxford University Press

Fung Chi Ming (2005) *Reluctant Heroes: Rickshaw Pullers in Hong Kong and Canton 1874-1954*, Hong Kong: Hong Kong University Press

Gartrell, Beverley (1984) 'Colonial Wives: villains or victims?' in Callan, Hilary & Ardener, Shirley (eds) *The Incorporated Wife* London: Croom Helm

Gillingham, Paul (1983) *At the Peak: Hong Kong between the wars*, Hong Kong: Macmillan

Gittens, Jean (1969) *Eastern Windows – Western Skies* Hong Kong: South China Morning Post Ltd

Goodman, William Meigh, Sir (1907) *Reminiscences of a Colonial Judge*, London: Kingsgate Press

Harrop, Phyllis (1943) *Hong Kong Incident*, London: Eyre & Spottiswoode

Hazzard, Shirley (2003) *The Great Fire*, New York: Picador

Historical and Statistical Abstract of the Colony of Hong Kong, 1841-1930, Third edition (1932), Hong Kong: Government Printers

Hoe, Susanna (1991) *The Private Life of Old Hong Kong*, Hong Kong: Oxford University Press

Holdsworth, May (2002) *Foreign Devils: expatriates in Hong Kong*, Hong Kong: Oxford University Press

(The) Hong Kong Daily Press (Friday May 4th 1923)

Hong Kong Hansard, (7 December 1891) Hong Kong Government Reports Online (1853-1941)

Hong Kong Museum of History (1994) *City of Victoria*, Hong Kong: Urban Council

Hosford, Stacilee F. (2002) *Gendered Exceptionalisms: American women in Hong Kong and Macao, 1830-2000*. Ph.D. Thesis, The University of Hong Kong

Hurley, R.C. (1920) *Handbook to the British Crown Colony of Hong Kong and Dependencies*. Hong Kong: Kelly and Walsh Limited

James, H.E.R (1892) *Correspondence* (loaned to the University of Hong Kong by his niece, Mrs T.D. Sorby)

Jarrett, Vincent H.G. *Old Hong Kong by 'Colonial'* – a series of articles on the history of Hong Kong taken from the *South China Morning Post*, 17 June 1933-13 April 1935

Kinchin Smith, Michael (1992) *The Irish Mays: a family history* (private publication)

Bibliography

Leiper, S. A. (1982) *A Yen for my Thoughts* Hong Kong: South China Morning Post Ltd

Lethbridge, H.J. (1970) 'Hong Kong Cadets, 1862-1941' *Journal of the Hong Kong Branch, Royal Asiatic Society*, Vol. 10, pp.36-56

Lethbridge, H.J. (1978) *Hong Kong: stability and change*: a collection of essays, Hong Kong: Oxford University Press

Luff, J. (1968) *Hong Kong Cavalcade*, Hong Kong: South China Morning Post Ltd.

Mattock, Katherine (1979) *This is Hong Kong: the story of Government House*. Hong Kong: Government Information Services

Mellor, B. (1980) *The University of Hong Kong: an informal history*. Hong Kong: Hong Kong University Press

Mellor, B. (1992) *Lugard in Hong Kong: empires, education and a Governor at work 1907-1912*, Hong Kong: Hong Kong University Press

Miners, N. (1987) *Hong Kong under Imperial Rule 1912-1941*, Hong Kong: Oxford University Press

Morrison, G.E. (1978) *The Correspondence of G.E. Morrison, Vol.2, edited by Lo Hui-min*, Cambridge: Cambridge University Press

Perham, Margery (1956) *Lugard: The Years of Authority 1898-1945*, London: Collins

Poynter, Mary A. (1921) *Around the Shores of Asia: a Diary of Travel from the Golden Horn to the Golden Gate*, London: Allen & Unwin

Roberts, R.E. (1939) *Portrait of Stella Benson*, London: Macmillan

Sayer, G.E., 1887-1962 (1975) *Hong Kong, 1862-1919: years of discretion*, edited and with additional notes by D.M.E. Evans, Hong Kong: Hong Kong University Press

Simpson, Sarah (2005) 'Honouring the Past: the early beginnings', www.worldywca1.org/common_concern/mar2005/cc125.pdf

Sinclair, Kevin (1994) Royal Hong Kong Police: 150th anniversary commemorative publication, 1844-1994, Hong Kong: Police Public Relations Branch, Royal Hong Kong Police Force

South China Weekly Post (1909) 'Birthday Honour Sir Francis Henry May, K.C.M.G.'

Spurr, Russell (1995) *Excellency: the Governors of Hong Kong*, Hong Kong: Formasia (Sir Henry May, pp.137-144)

(A) Staff Correspondent (1981) *Time to Remember [Series I-III] by A Staff Correspondent* (Newspaper clippings from the *South China Morning Post* 1964-1967)

Stark, Freya (1932) in Barker, E. & Stark, F. 'Women and the Service of Empire' *Contemporary Review, January, pp.54-61*

Strobel, Margaret (1991) *European Women and the Second British Empire*, Bloomington and Indianapolis: Indiana University Press

Trollope, Joanna (1983) *Britannia's Daughters: Women of the British Empire* Oxford: ISIS Publishing Ltd (large print edition 1995)

Tsang, S. (2004) *A Modern History of Hong Kong* Hong Kong: Hong Kong University Press

United Empire (March 1922) Obituary for Sir Henry May 'By one who knew him'

Warner, John (1981) *Hong Kong Illustrated: views and news 1840-1890*. Hong Kong: John Warner Publications

Welsh, Frank (1993) *A History of Hong Kong*, London: Harper-Collins

Whitworth, Phoebe (2001) *View from the Peak*, Second Edition, Cambridge: Cambridge University Press, (First published in 1966)

Who Was Who, a companion to Who's Who, containing the biographies of those who died 1897 – 1915 (Vol. 1), London: Adam & Charles Black

Who's Who in the Far East 1906-7, Hong Kong: China Mail

Wiltshire, Trea (1989) 'Hong Kong – striding with the bold effrontery of Empire' in *Great Cities of the World: Old Hong Kong*, Hong Kong: Formasia

Wordie, Jason (2002) *Streets: Exploring Hong Kong Island*, Hong Kong: Hong Kong University Press

Wright, A. & Cartwright, H.A. (eds.) (1908) *Twentieth Century Impressions of Hong Kong: history, people, commerce, industries and resources*. Reprinted 1990 Singapore: Graham Brash

www.lcsd.gov.hk/CE/Museum/Monument/eng/declared

YWCA Report 1912 C.O.129/410 Public Record Office, London

List of Illustrations

Front	The main room in 1916 *reproduced by courtesy of the Public Records Office*
II	Helena May at Mountain Lodge 1915 *reproduced by courtesy of the Public Records Office*
VI	The Military Cantonment, Victoria (1880) *reproduced by courtesy of the Hong Kong Museum of History*
IX	Stonework above the entrance, with the engraved name now missing
XI	Rooftop and window details on the east side of the building
XII	Architectural feature
XIV	Helena and Henry May at Mountain Lodge *reproduced by courtesy of the Public Records Office*
1	Helena in mourning dress in 1873 *reproduced by courtesy of Lorna Headlam-Morley*
3	Helena just before she came to Hong Kong in 1890 *reproduced by courtesy of Timothy Whitworth*
5	Bahar Lodge, 28 Mount Austin Road *reproduced by courtesy of the Public Records Office*
7	View of the Peak Tram with a house on the left that is probably Ligoniel *reproduced by courtesy of Timothy Whitworth*
8	Mountain Lodge 1912 *reproduced by courtesy of the Public Records Office*
9	The daughters and Ah Soo (Sooey) Clare Hall, 1905 *reproduced by courtesy of the Public Records Office*
12	Helena, Henry and daughters c. 1910 *reproduced by courtesy of the Public Records Office*
17	Statue of Henry May *reproduced by courtesy of the Museum of History*
18	Statue Square (1925) *reproduced by courtesy of the Museum of History*
20	Helena and her grandchildren at Clare Priory 1926 *reproduced by the May Family*
22-23	Photographs of Helena and family members in the 1890s *reproduced by courtesy of Christopher Bailey, Picture This Gallery*
24	Helena and the Voluntary Aid Detachment during the First World War *reproduced by courtesy of the Public Records Office*
28	Students and teachers with Lady May at Mountain Lodge around 1912 *reproduced by courtesy of St Stephen's Girls' School*
30	Inscription in the bible presented to Helena in 1910 *reproduced by courtesy of Veronica Johnston*
31	YWCA report 1912 with Helena's name on cover *reproduced by courtesy of the National Archives, Kew, UK*
34	Photograph of Helena and other ladies packing bandages *reproduced by courtesy of the Public Records Office*
37	Speeches at the opening ceremony *reproduced by courtesy of the Public Records Office*
38	The opening of the building *reproduced by courtesy of the Public Records Office*
39	Ellis Kadoorie, Henry May and Ho Kom Tong at the opening *reproduced by courtesy of the Public Records Office*
42-43	Feature photographs – bell and speaking tube, mail rack, letterbox on the door and Blue Room detail
44	Early view of the Helena May *reproduced by courtesy of the Public Records Office*
45	The Peak Tram, covered nullah and rear of the Helena May 1918 *reproduced by courtesy of the Public Records Office*
56-57	Features of the library inside and out
63	Map of Victoria 1936 *reproduced by courtesy of the Public Records Office*
65	Japanese book pocket reproduced by courtesy of the University of Hong Kong Library
66-67	Feature photographs – Helena May signs
68	The Helena May and Victoria taken by Hedda Morrison reproduced by courtesy of Harvard-Yenching Library at Harvard University and Edward Stokes
69	One of the original blackwood seats in the entrance hall

List of Illustrations

72	The exterior in 1951 *reproduced by courtesy of Rosemary Inglis*
73	Architectural features including residents' balcony on the west side
79	Collage of photographs *reproduced by courtesy of Rosemary Inglis*
80	The laundry in the garden and St Joseph's college opposite *reproduced by courtesy of the Public Records Office*
82	Carol Bateman *reproduced by courtesy of Alistair Stewart*
85	The ballet school *reproduced by courtesy of Alistair Stewart*
88	Aerial photograph taken in 1963 *reproduced by courtesy of St Joseph's College*
92	Retirement presentation *reproduced by courtesy of the Hong Kong Standard*
96-97	Plan of the ground floor of the Helena May after the library moved downstairs
98	Aerial photograph taken from the Cheung Kong Centre *reproduced by courtesy of Colin Day*
100	Mr Sinn's photograph of the exterior of the building
101	A Helena May trip to the New Territories with Dr Solomon Bard *reproduced by courtesy of Esther Morris*
105	Photographs taken by Helena May members and staff at various functions
112-113	Feature photographs – the garden and other outside areas
Inside flap	Certificate naming the exterior facade of the Helena May as a Declared Monument
Back	View of the east side of the Helena May 1916

The May Collection at the Public Records Office (PRO) comprises approximately 630 photographs taken between 1912 and 1919. They were presented to the PRO by one of Helena and Henry's daughters, Iris Johnston.

Index

Ah Soo (Sooey) **9**
Anderson, Shaemus (James) O'Gorman 48
Angus, Marjorie 50, 54, 55
Annett, Mrs Mabel 71
Annexe, The 81, 82, 84, 88;
opening 86; closing 89; subletting 91, 92; reopening as The Court 94;
Bahar Lodge 5, 7
Bard, Solomon 100, **101**
Barker Road 3
Barker, Digby Hildyard 1, 3,
Barker, Frances Isabella (née Murray) 1, 2
Barker, Mary Caroline (Carrie) 1, 3, 15
Barker, Sir George Digby 1, 2, 3
Barrington, Olivia 3
Bateman Carol (Howell) 75, 76, **82**, 83, 86
use of hall 80, 81, 87; retirement 89
Benson, Stella (Mrs James Anderson) 47, 53
Bent, Marjory **105**, 109
Black, Mrs G.D.R. 60, 69, 74
Blake, Sir Henry 8
Blue Book for the Year 1912 13
Bodichon, Barbara 25
Bowes-Smith, Aubrey M. 53, 58
Bowes-Smith, K. Marjory 58
Bowring, Mrs 82
Boxer Rebellion 7, 16, 39
Bray, Denis 77, 109
Bray, Marjorie (née Bottomley) 77, 89, 99, 101, **105**, 106, 109; Council Chairman 106
British Women's Emigration Association 26
Buttifant, Gail 99, 110
Campbell, Joan 82, 84, **85**, 86, 90, 94, **105**, 109;
succeeds Carol Bateman, 89
Campbell, Mrs Mary 71
Canossian Convent 27
Carden, Miss 28
Cassidy, Mrs Margery 71
Census, see Population
Central Police Station 4, 5, 7, 17
Chabot, Letty Chiu 106, 108
Chan Kai Ming 34, 37, 40
China Mail 29
Church Missionary Society (CMS) 27, 28
City Hall Work Party 46
Clare Hall 1, 9, 20
Clare Priory 1 3, 17, 19, 20
Clark, Sir Francis 15
Clementi, Lady Penelope (née Eyres) 11, 51, 52, 54, 55
Clementi, Sir Cecil 4, 11, 15, 51
Collins, Dorothy 75, 88, **105**
Colonial Nursing Association 26
Connell, Annelise 86, 88, 107
Coppock, Miss 33
Cote, Elizabeth 110
Cotton Tree Drive (Kapok Drive) 87, 93
Court, The 99, 106, 109, 111
opening 94; redevelopment 103, 107
Dalton, Major General James Cecil 3
de Fonblanque, Anne, **20**
de Fonblanque, Mary **20**
de Fonblanque, Philip 16
Denison, Ram & Gibbs 15, 33, 38
Dunbar, Mrs Elsie 71
Duncan, Mary 4, 19
Eltringham, Shirley 101
Elwes, Katherine (Katie) Weston 3
Everett, Mrs Margery 71
Eyre Diocesan Refuge 45
Eyre, Lucy 27, 29, 31, 36
and founding of YWCA 30, 32
Eyres, Dorothy 11
Eyres, Penelope (see Clementi)
Faber, Mrs Gwen 81, 82
Faber, S.E. 82, 84
Fairlee 27
Female Education Society (FES) 27
Flagstaff House (Headquarter House) 3
Fleming, Mrs Katherine 71
Garrett, Elizabeth 25
Girl Guides 35, 38, 45
Gittens, Billy 60
Gittens, Jean 60, 69, 77
Gourgey, Ivor 37, 40
Great Fire,The 76
Griffin, Miss 28, 29
Griffiths, Dr 81
Grist, Evelyn 55
Gundersen, Mrs M. 71
Hamper, Agnes 27, 30
Hampshire, Liz 104
Han Suyin 76
Hazlerigg, Hon. T.M 74
Hazzard, Shirley 76, **105**
Headlam-Morley, Lorna (née Kinchin Smith) 19, **20**
Heep Yunn School 27, 28
Heitmeyer, Thelma 100
Helena May (Institute) 15, 33, 35, 41; opening of, 36-38, 40; improvements 49; Kowloon premises 51-52, 54; librarian appointed 51, 53, 99; as Japanese Public Library 62-65; de-requisitioning 70; re-incorporation 70-71; expansion 84; Annexe opens 86; 50th anniversary 87; financial deficit 89; negative press 91, 92, 93; typhoon damage 92, the Court opens 94; change of name 95; Declared Monument 103, redevelopment of the Court 103-4
Helena May Institute for Women 33
Helena, Princess 1, 30

INDEX

Hildesheim Home 27
Ho Fook 18, 39
Ho Kom Tong 32, 36
as benefactor 18, 33, 37, 38, 39
Ho, Stella Pak-Ngor 108
Ho Tung, Sir Robert 8, 16, 18, 28, 35, 39, 51
relatives of 17, 49, 69, 71; benefactor 37, 39, 40
Ho Tung, Victoria 17
Ho Yum Chuen 70, 92
Ho, Mrs Victoria 17
Hoare, Bishop 9
Hoe, Susanna 30, 32
Hong Kong Association of (Women) War Workers 45, 46
Hong Kong Benevolent Society (HKBS) 29, 32
Hong Kong Cadets 4
Hong Kong Defence Corps 16
Hong Kong Daily Press 2, 18
Hong Kong Jockey Club 77, 83, 84, 86
Hongkong News 65
Hong Kong Nursing Institution 27
Hong Kong Refuge for Chinese Women and Girls 27, 29
Hong Kong Telegraph 2, 54
Japanese occupation of Hong Kong 3, 16, 40, 45, 47, 61, 62
Johnston, Francis 91
Johnston, Veronica 20, 87
Kadoorie, Lady Muriel 60, 100, **105**
Kadoorie, Sir Ellis 33-34, 40, 49, 108
letter to Helena 32, 33; opening ceremony 36-38;
as benefactor 32, 34, 38,49 52
Kemp, Mrs J.H. 47
Kennedy-Skipton, Mrs 59
Keswick, Hon. J.J. 4
Kinchin Smith, Lorna (see Headlam-Morley)
Kinchin Smith, Michael 4, 19, **20**
Kinnaird, Mary Jane 25
Kom Tong Hall 39, 108
Kowloon-Canton Railway 12
Ladies Recreation Club 26
Lander, Bishop 32
Lander, Margaret 30
Lane, Winsome 99, 101
Larry Tam & Associates 104
Lau Chu Pak 6, 34, 37, 40, 49
Lee, Rosemary 101, **101**
Lee Wing Kee 79, 90, 100
Leigh and Orange 104
Li Hong-hung 14
Ligoniel 7, 13
Lincolne, Matilda 29
Lo, Marge 110
Lowe, Bingham & Matthews 69, 70, 83
Lugard, Lady Flora (née Shaw) 9, 10, 29
Lugard, Sir Frederick 9-10, 11, 15, 19, 29
Mackennal, Sir Bertram 18
Mackenzie, Mrs A. 47
Many Splendoured Thing, A 76
Married Women's Property Ordinance 28
Matheson, Margery 70, 71, 78, 81, 84
Matilda Hospital 29, 34
May Hall 15
May, Charlotte Phoebe 4
May, Dione 4, 7, 19,
May, Edward, 4
May, Rt. Hon. George A.C. 3
May, Gould 4, 6, 20
May, Helena Augusta Victoria (nee Barker)
early life and marriage 2-4,; and Clare Priory, 3, 17, 19; farewell presentation 12-13, 30; return to England 17; death of 20; and local organisations, 27, 29, 35; and YWCA 30, 31
May, Iris 20, 38. 46, 87
May, Michael 4, 19
May, Phoebe 12, 15, 20
birth 6; and George Whitworth 3, 9; *View from the Peak* 3, 4, 5, 6, 7, 8; Lugard letter 11; farewell presentation to Helena 12; Fiji 13; and assassination attempt 14; donates Lady Chapel 16
May, Rt. Hon. George A.C. 3
May, Sir Henry
birth 3, early life and marriage 4; family life 6; and YMCA 7, 19; knighthood 11; acting Governor of Hong Kong 8, 11; Colonial Secretary 9; Governor of Fiji 12 ; Governor of Hong Kong 13; assassination attempt 13-14 ; sense of duty 16; departure from Hong Kong 17; statue of 17, 18; death of 17; resignation as Governor 17, 46
May, Stella 4, 5, 9, 11, 15, 19
birth 5; engagement 16; and Roman Catholicism 21
May, Stella Millicent, 4
McLean Robyn, 101
Meath, Lady 29
Miller, Mrs M.C. 90
Ministering Children's League, Hong Kong 27, 29, 58
Ministering League 58
Mody, Hormusjee Navrotjee 29
Moore, Mrs A.D. 89
Morris, Esther 100, **105**
Morrison, G.E. 14, 16
Mother's Union Work Party 46
Mountain Lodge 8, 11, 14, 16, 28
Museum of Tea Ware 3
Nathan, Sir Matthew 8, 9
Ng, Mei Ling 90
Nigel, Mr 89
Nursing Detachment of Hong Kong Volunteers 60
Opium 3, 9, 10
Orde, Lady Eileen 53
Osmaston, Margaret 20, 77, 101, 104

INDEX

Our Little Bit Society 46
Parker, Mrs 99
Patten, Lavender 104, **105**
Peak Hotel 13, 16
Pearl Harbour 60
Piggott, (Lady) Mabel 26, 27
Plague 5, 15, 26, 39
Po Leung Kok 27
Pollock, H.E., K.C. 30, 36
Pollock, Mrs H.E. 47
Population, in 1916 41; in 1921 48; in 1931 54; in 1951 78; in 1961 86; in 1971 92; in 1981 100; in 1991 102; in 2006 111
Poynter, Mary 35
Prostitutes 41, 49, 53, 54, 61
Public Works Department 61
Queen Alexandra's Imperial Military Nursing Service 27
Queen Mary's Needlework Guild 45, 46
Rees Davies, Lady 47
Rees Davies, Sir William 16, 36
Rensuke, Lt. Gen. Isogai 61
Ride, L.T. 58
Robarts, Emma 25
Rowell, Mrs Edith 71
SARS 108
Scout Association , The 92, 94
Shaw, Flora, see Lugard
Simpson, Betty 109
Singh, Kala 14
Singh, Vijai 102, 103, 104
Sinn, Mr 99
Society for Overseas Settlement of Women Annual Report 51
So Hoi. 79
South China Morning Post 27, 34, 36-8, 40
South China Weekly Post 11
Southorn, Lady 55, 58
Specialist Academy 101
St John's Cathedral 2, 4, 16
St Stephen's Girls College 27, 28
St Stephen's Preparatory College 28
Stabb, Mrs 47
Staff, loyalty of 70, 75, 89, 92, 108
Stafford, Mrs 91
Stewart, Alistair 89
Stewart, Pat **85**, 89
Stoiche, Leanne 111
Strickland, Anthea 101
Suffragettes 34, 35
Sun Yat Sen 39, 51
Sykes, Mrs Ivy 71
Tam, Larry & Associates 104
Tang Shiu Kin 54
The Lady 101
Thomson, A.M. 13
Tiananmen Square 102
Toshiko Eto 61
Tratman, Mrs 55
Trollope, Joanne 9
Tsang, Selina, 111, **105**
Tung, Betty 104, **105**
University of Hong Kong 10, 15, 29, 40, 49, 58
Victoria Barracks 2, 3
Victoria British School 35
Victoria Home and Orphanage 27-8
Victoria Prison 4
View from the Peak 3
Wade, Eileen 83, 90, 91
Watson, Hon. Mr M.M. 74
Welsh, Frank 19
Wesleyan Church Work Party 46
Whitworth, Andrew 20
Whitworth, George 3, 9
Whitworth, Phoebe, see Phoebe May
Whitworth, Timothy 20
Winchester International School 101
Wolfe, Agnes 55
Woo, Mrs Dorothy 71
Wright, Mrs Beth 71
YMCA 7, 19
Youde, Lady 100, 101
Young, Lady 70, 71, 74, 75
Young, Sir Mark 59, 69
Yue, Rosanna 89, **105**
YWCA Hong Kong 28, 33, 34, 38, 71, 76, 89, 90; founded, 30, 47; and Lucy Eyre, 30, 31, 32
YWCA, London 25